Study Guide

to accompany

Social Psychology

Seventh Edition

David G. Myers
Hope College

Prepared by
Martin Bolt
Calvin College

Boston   Burr Ridge, IL   Dubuque, IA   Madison, WI   New York   San Francisco   St. Louis
Bangkok   Bogotá   Caracas   Kuala Lumpur   Lisbon   London   Madrid   Mexico City
Milan   Montreal   New Delhi   Santiago   Seoul   Singapore   Sydney   Taipei   Toronto

McGraw-Hill Higher Education

A Division of The McGraw-Hill Companies

Study Guide to accompany
SOCIAL PSYCHOLOGY, SEVENTH EDITION
DAVID G. MYERS

Published by McGraw-Hill Higher Education, an imprint of The McGraw-Hill Companies, Inc.,
1221 Avenue of the Americas, New York, NY 10020. Copyright © The McGraw-Hill Companies,
Inc., 2002, 1999, 1996, 1993, 1990, 1987, 1983. All rights reserved.

2 3 4 5 6 7 8 9 0 VNH VNH 0 3 2

ISBN 0-07-241395-6

www.mhhe.com

CONTENTS

INTRODUCTION: HOW TO USE THIS STUDY GUIDE

This study guide is designed to help you master the material presented in David G. Myers' Social Psychology, seventh edition. It will also test your comprehension of text material and provide a review for class examination. Each chapter in the study guide corresponds to a text chapter and is organized into the following sections:

Chapter Objectives. These highlight what you should learn from a careful study of the text and thus provide a basis for self-evaluation. Since the list of objectives also gives an overview of the chapter's major ideas and organization, you may want to review them before reading the chapter.

Chapter Review. The fill-in-the-blank summary is a review of the chapter's major ideas. The subheadings parallel those in the text, and you may choose either to fill in the blanks after you have read the respective section in the text, or wait until you have finished the entire chapter. Note that the correct answers are found in the Answer Key toward the end of each chapter. This review also provides a quick refresher just before a class examination.

Matching Terms. This exercise provides a list of concepts you should be familiar with after studying the chapter. Close attention to the definitions provided in the text margin will promote your mastery of the chapter's key terms.

True-False Review. These items along with the multiple-choice questions that follow offer a means of assessing your progress in mastering the chapter's content. They also provide a review of some of the chapter's major ideas.

Multiple-Choice Practice Test. Multiple-choice items are commonly used in classroom tests and you may want to wait until you feel you are adequately prepared to take a regular examination before completing this section as practice. Most of the items assess your knowledge of the chapter's basic content. A few challenge you to go beyond the information presented in the text and apply it to new problems and situations.

Short Essay Questions. Your ability to answer these will provide a good indication of whether you have mastered the chapter objectives.

Answer Key. This gives the correct responses for the chapter review, matching, true-false, and multiple-choice exercises. Checking your answers will reveal sections of the chapter that may require additional review.

CHAPTER 1

INTRODUCING SOCIAL PSYCHOLOGY

CHAPTER OBJECTIVES

After completing your study of this chapter you should be able to:

1. Define social psychology and give examples of the discipline's central concerns.

2. Identify similarities and differences between social psychology and the other disciplines that study human nature.

3. Indicate how the personal values of social psychologists penetrate their work.

4. Discuss the nature and implications of the "hindsight bias" for social psychology.

5. Explain the general nature and purpose of a theory.

6. Describe two major research methods used in social psychology and state the advantages and disadvantages of each.

7. Identify ethical standards that govern social-psychological research.

CHAPTER REVIEW

Supply the words necessary to complete each of the following statements.

1. Social psychology is the ___Scientific___ study of how people think about, ___influence___, and relate to one another. It is still a ___young___ discipline with the first social psychology experiments being reported just a ___century (1898)___ ago.

SOCIAL PSYCHOLOGY AND RELATED DISCIPLINES

2. Most sociologists study _groups_, while social psychologists are usually interested in studying average _individuals_. In comparison to the sociologist, the social psychologist makes greater use of the _Experimental_ method.

3. Compared to personality psychology, social psychology focuses less attention on _differences_ between individuals, and has a _Shorter_ history.

4. _evolutionary_ psychologists show how natural selection may predispose our social behavior. Social _psychologist_ remind us that we must consider biological influences on loving and hating.

5. The disciplines that study human nature provide different _perspectives_ of explanation that _Compliment_ rather than contradict one another.

SOCIAL PSYCHOLOGY AND HUMAN VALUES

6. Social psychologists' personal _values_ penetrate their work in obvious ways like their _Choice_ of research topics.

7. In addition there is a growing awareness that science is not as purely _Objective_ as commonly thought. The scientists' _____ control their interpretations and _____ are hidden in the concepts and labels of social psychology. Scientists are guilty of the _____ fallacy when they define what is good in terms of what is observable.

I KNEW IT ALL ALONG: IS SOCIAL PSYCHOLOGY SIMPLY COMMON SENSE?

8. The _____ bias is the tendency to exaggerate one's ability to have foreseen how something turned out after learning the outcome and may explain why social psychology's findings often seem like _____.

HOW WE DO SOCIAL PSYCHOLOGY

9. Social psychologists organize their ideas and findings into _____ that both explain and _____ observed events.

10. Most social psychological research is conducted either in the_____ or in the _____ and is either _____ or _____.

11. The great strength of correlational research is that it tends to occur in _____ settings where it can examine important factors that cannot be _____ in the laboratory. Correlational research can tell us whether two variables are associated but cannot provide _____ explanations.

2

12. Survey researchers obtain a representative group by taking a _____ in which every person in the total group has an equal chance of being chosen to participate. About _____ randomly selected participants will enable the researcher to be 95 percent confident of describing the entire population within an error margin of 3 percent or less. Four potentially biasing influences on surveys are _____ samples, the _____ in which questions are asked, the _____ options, and the _____ of the questions.

13. Two essential ingredients of every social-psychological experiment are _____ and _____ assignment. Researchers often walk a tightrope in designing experiments that will be involving yet _____.

MATCHING TERMS

Write the letter of the correct term from the right before the appropriate number on the left

_____ 1. A cue in an experiment that tells the participant what behavior is expected.

_____ 2. The study of the naturally occurring relationships among variables.

_____ 3. An integrated set of principles that explain and predict observed events.

_____ 4. Defining what is good in terms of what is observable.

_____ 5. Research done in natural, real-life settings outside the laboratory.

_____ 6. Placing participants in an experiment such that each has an equal chance of being in a given condition.

_____ 7. Research participants must be told enough to enable them to choose whether they wish to participate.

_____ 8. Seeks clues to cause-effect relationships by manipulating one or factors while controlling others.

_____ 9. Every person in the group has had an equal chance of being chosen to participate in a study.

_____ 10. The tendency to exaggerate one's ability to have foreseen how something turned out, after learning the outcome.

_____ 11. Extent to which an experiment is super-ficially similar to everyday situations.

_____ 12. Extent to which an experiment absorbs and involves its participants.

_____ 13. Enduring behaviors and ideas shared by a large group of people and transmitted from one generation to the next.

a. naturalistic fallacy

b. random assignment

c. correlational research

d. mundane realism

e. random sample

f. experimental realism

g. hindsight bias

h. field research

i. experimental research

j. demand characteristic

k. informed consent

l. culture

m. theory

4

TRUE-FALSE REVIEW

Circle T if the statement is true and F if it is false.

T F 1. The first social psychology experiments were reported in the 1930s.

T F 2. In comparison to sociologists, social psychologists are more interested in studying the individual.

T F 3. Contemporary social psychology emphasizes the power of the situation and downplays the contribution of the person to social behavior.

T F 4. In comparison to social psychologists, personality psychologists have a special concern for the similarities between individuals.

T F 5. To the degree social psychologists are successful in explaining human behavior, other disciplines become less important.

T F 6. Social psychology's ultimate goal is to explain the purpose of human life.

T F 7. Social representations are our most important but least examined convictions.

T F 8. A study of the Princeton-Dartmouth football game showed how our opinions control our interpretations.

T F 9. The "I-Knew-It-All-Along" phenomenon provides one example of the naturalistic fallacy.

T F 10. Social psychologists have investigated how values are formed and how they can be changed.

T F 11. Hidden value judgments are more common in psychology than in sociology.

T F 12. Random assignment is an important feature of well-done surveys.

T F 13. A total of 1200 randomly selected participants will enable a survey researcher to be 95 percent confident of describing the entire population of a country with an error margin of 3 percent or less.

T F 14. The order in which questions are asked can influence respondents' answers in a survey.

T F 15. There are at least three possible explanations for every correlational finding.

T F 16. Contemporary social psychology recognizes the importance of cognition in understanding social behavior.

T F 17. The experimental method enables researchers to answer questions about causal relationships.

T F 18. The correlational method is used in about one-half of social-psychological research studies.

T F 19. Demand characteristics are cues in an experiment that tell the participant what behavior is expected.

T F 20. An experiment has mundane realism if it absorbs and involves its participants.

T F 21. One ethical principle advocated by the American Psychological Association is that investigators treat information about the individual research participants confidentially.

T F 22. Theories are most frequently discarded because they have been falsified.

T F 23. A good theory makes clear predictions that can be used to confirm or modify the theory.

T F 24. The findings of social psychology typically prove common sense ideas are wrong.

T F 25. Hindsight bias is conducive to arrogance—an overestimation of our own intellectual powers.

MULTIPLE-CHOICE PRACTICE TEST

Circle the correct letter.

1. Social psychology is the scientific study of how people _____, _____, and _____ one another.

    a. understand, feel about, act toward
    b. perceive, think about, act toward
    c. think about, influence, relate to
    d. observe, influence, conflict with

2. Social psychology began to emerge as the vibrant field it is today during

    a. the depression of the early 1930s when researchers examined the effects of deprivation on aggression and altruism
    b. World War I when psychologists conducted studies of social conflict and cooperation
    c. World War II when researchers contributed studies of persuasion and soldier morale
    d. the Korean War when psychologists examined the effects of brainwashing on prisoners of war

3. In comparison to the sociologist, the social psychologist

   a. is more likely to study the social causes of behavior
   b. is more likely to study individuals than groups
   c. gives less attention to our internal functioning
   d. relies more heavily on correlational research

4. In comparison to personality psychology, social psychology

   a. has a shorter history
   b. is more concerned with the biological causes of behavior
   c. is more likely to use case studies in theory development
   d. has greater concern for differences between individuals

5. In comparison to personality psychology, social psychology

   a. focuses more on our common humanity
   b. has more famous, well-known theorists
   c. is an older specialty within the discipline of psychology
   d. provides more "grand" or comprehensive theories of human functioning

6. According to the text, which word best describes the relationship between different disciplines that study behavior?

   a. supplementary   c. complementary
   b. contradictory   d. competing

7. The text states that as a scientific discipline, social psychology

   a. is superior to those disciplines that assume a more subjective approach to the study of human nature
   b. can assist in explaining the meaning of life
   c. is <u>one</u> perspective from which we can view and better understand human nature
   d. offers explanations for human nature that often contradict the claims of other disciplines

8. Most social-psychological research is conducted either in the field or in the _____ and is either correlational or _____.

   a. clinic; survey   c. laboratory; survey
   b. laboratory; experimental d. clinic; experimental

9. Survey researchers obtain a representative group

   a. through random assignment
   b. by selecting at least 2000 respondents to be interviewed
   c. by taking a random sample
   d. either through telephone books or automobile registrations

10. The great strength of _____ is that it tends to occur in real-world settings where it can examine questions regarding important factors like race, sex, and social status.

   a. correlational research
   b. field experimentation
   c. laboratory experimentation
   d. quasi-experimentation

11. Which of the following distinguishes the correlational method from experimentation?

   a. the correlational method uses a smaller group of subjects
   b. the correlational method enables researchers to study social attitudes
   c. no attempt is made to systematically manipulate one or more factors with the correlational method
   d. the findings from the correlational method are more likely to be contaminated by the experimenter's values

12. To determine whether changing one variable (like education) will produce changes in another (like income), we need to conduct _____ research.

   a. survey   c. experimental
   b. correlational   d. statistical

13. "Random assignment" means that each person taking part in an experiment must
   a. have an equal chance of being in a given condition in the experiment
   b. be assigned to all the conditions of the experimental treatment
   c. be randomly selected from the larger population
   d. be given random responses to the experimenter's questions

14. An experiment has mundane realism if

   a. the experimental task is similar to tasks in everyday life
   b. it involves and absorbs people
   c. it is conducted in the field
   d. the experimenter deceives subjects

15. The experimental factor that the experimenter manipulates is called the _____ variable.

   a. dependent   c. independent
   b. control   d. experimental

16. In an experiment, the variable being measured is called the _____ variable.

   a. control   c. experimental
   b. independent   d. dependent

17. The experimental method is used in about _____ of all social-psychological research studies.

    a. one-fourth
    b. one-half
    c. three-fourths
    d. nine-tenths

18. Random assignment is necessary to

    a. insure mundane realism
    b. insure informed consent
    c. rule out pre-existing differences between subjects in different experimental conditions
    d. avoid the naturalistic fallacy

19. Which of the following is false according to the text?

    a. experimenters standardize their instructions to subjects to minimize demand characteristics
    b. the American Psychological Association has developed a number of ethical principles to guide investigators
    c. informed consent is an important ethical principle to be followed in conducting research
    d. deception should never be used in conducting research

20. Hypotheses are best characterized as

    a. axioms
    b. principles
    c. predictions
    d. conclusions

21. According to the text, _____ tends to make people overconfident about the validity of their judgments and predictions.

    a. the fundamental attribution error
    b. illusory correlation
    c. the naturalistic fallacy
    d. the hindsight bias

22. In an experimental study of the effects of failure on self-esteem, self-esteem would be the

    a. control condition
    b. independent variable
    c. dependent variable
    d. experimental condition

23. Widely held ideas and values that we take for granted and that help us make sense of our world are called

    a. pluralistic assumptions
    b. cultural traditions
    c. social heuristics
    d. social representations

24. The author of the text suggests that adjectives such as "self-actualized," "mature," and "well-adjusted" demonstrate

   a. how psychological concepts have hidden values
   b. how psychological concepts are individualistic
   c. an inordinate concern with mental health
   d. how personality psychologists are more influential than social psychologists

25. According to the text, the fact that human thinking always involves interpretation

   a. provides a valid reason for dismissing science
   b. is precisely why we need scientific analysis
   c. is a reason for preferring experimental over correlational research
   d. has been more frequently recognized by those in the sciences than by those in the humanities

26. How prior opinions control interpretations is illustrated by

   a. Hastorf and Cantril's study of reactions to the Princeton-Dartmouth football game
   b. Slovic and Fischhoff's study of the "I-Knew-It-All-Along" phenomenon
   c. the Literary Digest's erroneous prediction of the winner of the 1936 presidential election
   d. Bachman and O'Malley's study of the relationship between self-esteem and achievement

27. The naturalistic fallacy provides an example of

   a. the hindsight bias
   b. how values penetrate the work of the scientist
   c. how common sense notions are often wrong
   d. how naturalistic observation is unable to answer questions about cause-effect relationships

28. Modern social psychology emphasizes

   a. the power of the situation
   b. the power of the person
   c. the importance of cognition
   d. all of the above

29. Several psychologists have recently challenged the idea that

   a. high self-esteem produces academic achievement
   b. the ingredients of loneliness are the same in different cultures
   c. parental education predicts children's achievement
   d. televised violence is a cause of children's aggressive behavior

30. Who of the following is most likely to study how religious attitudes develop within the typical individual?

a. a sociologist
b. a social worker
c. a social psychologist
d. a theologian

31. Who of the following would be most likely to study how the political attitudes of middle-class people differ from those of lower-class people?

a. a personality psychologist
b. a social psychologist
c. a social biologist
d. a sociologist

32. You would like to know the relationship between the number of psychology courses people take and their interpersonal sensitivity. You survey college students to determine how much psychology they have taken and then have them complete a test of social sensitivity. Finally you plot the relationship. This is an example of

a. a laboratory experiment
b. a field experiment
c. a correlational study
d. participant observation

33. The telephone company wants to survey its 100,000 customers. Four proposals for sampling the customers are being considered. Which would you recommend?

a. interview every 75th person listed in the telephone directory
b. mail a questionnaire to all 100,000 customers and assume at least 1200 will respond
c. interview the people in every 50th residence from a postal listing of all addresses
d. interview those 1,000 persons with the highest phone bills

34. A research psychologist manipulates the level of fear in human subjects in the laboratory and then examines what effect the different levels of fear have on the subjects' reaction times. In this study, reaction time is the _____ variable.

a. dependent
b. correlational
c. independent
d. experimental

35. In conducting a study of conformity, the experimenters decide to tape-record the instructions that are to be presented to all subjects. Their decision is most likely an attempt to minimize the effect of

a. hindsight bias
b. mundane realism
c. naturalistic fallacy
d. demand characteristics

36. A researcher finds that Americans bathe on the average of once a day. He concludes that an educational program is necessary to encourage more frequent bathing by those who bathe less than once a day. The researcher is probably guilty of

    a. hindsight bias
    b. the "I-Knew-It-All-Along" phenomenon
    c. illusory correlation
    d. the naturalistic fallacy

37. Which of the following research methods would be most effective in demonstrating that the presence of others improves our performance of a task?

    a. an experiment   c. a survey
    b. a correlational study   d. a field study

38. Which of the following techniques would be the most effective way of investigating the relationship between the political preferences and the age of American citizens?

    a. an experiment   c. a correlational study
    b. a case study   d. participant observation

39. A negative correlation between degree of wealth and the likelihood of being involved in criminal activity would indicate that

    a. poverty makes people more likely to commit a crime
    b. the poor are more likely to be involved in criminal activity than are the wealthy
    c. being involved in criminal activity usually prevents people from accumulating wealth
    d. all of the above are necessarily true

40. In a research study investigating the effects of stress on the desire to affiliate, half of the participants complete an easy test of mental ability and half complete a difficult test. What technique should the investigators use to ensure that any post-test differences in the group's desire to affiliate actually result from the differences in test difficulty?

    a. random sampling   c. replication
    b. random assignment   d. correlational measurement

SHORT ESSAY QUESTIONS

Answer the following questions in the space provided.

1. Define social psychology.

2. Briefly describe how social psychology differs from sociology and from personality psychology.

3. What is the relationship between the various disciplines that study human behavior?

4. What is the "I-Knew-It-All-Along" phenomenon? What are its implications for social psychology?

5. Briefly describe three ways in which the personal values of social psychologists penetrate their work.

6. Describe two important functions of a theory.

7. Describe the differences between a correlational study and an experimental study.

8. What ethical problems do social psychologists encounter in conducting research? How have these problems been addressed?

ANSWER KEY

Chapter Review

1. scientific
    influence
    young
    century

2. groups
    individuals
    experimental

3. differences
    shorter

4. Evolutionary
    neuroscientists

5. levels
    complement

6. values
    choice

7. objective
    preconceptions
    values
    naturalistic

8. hindsight
    common sense

9. theories
    predict

10. laboratory
    field
    correlational
    experimental

11. real-world
    manipulated
    cause-effect

12. random sample
    1200
    unrepresentative
    order
    response
    wording

13. control
    random
    ethical

Matching Terms

1.	j	7.	k
2.	c	8.	i
3.	m	9.	e
4.	a	10.	g
5.	h	11.	d
6.	b	12.	f
		13.	l

True-False Review

1.	F	14.	T
2.	T	15.	T
3.	F	16.	T
4.	F	17.	T
5.	F	18.	F
6.	F	19.	T
7.	T	20.	F
8.	T	21.	T
9.	F	22.	F
10.	T	23.	T
11.	F	24.	F
12.	F	25.	T
13.	T		

Multiple-Choice Practice Test

1.	c	21.	d
2.	c	22.	c
3.	b	23.	d
4.	a	24.	a
5.	a	25.	b
6.	c	26.	a
7.	c	27.	b
8.	b	28.	d
9.	c	29.	a
10.	a	30.	c
11.	c	31.	d
12.	c	32.	c
13.	a	33.	a
14.	a	34.	a
15.	c	35.	d
16.	d	36.	d
17.	c	37.	a
18.	c	38.	c
19.	d	39.	b
20.	c	40.	b

CHAPTER 2

THE SELF IN A SOCIAL WORLD

CHAPTER OBJECTIVES

After completing your study of this chapter you should be able to:

1. Describe the nature of our self-concept and discuss how our beliefs about ourselves influence our thoughts and actions.

2. Describe the factors that shape our self-concept.

3. Discuss research findings regarding the accuracy of our self-knowledge.

4. Define self-efficacy and explain its relationship to behavior.

5. Give several examples of the self-serving bias and discuss why people perceive themselves in self-enhancing ways.

6. Describe how the self-serving bias can be adaptive but also maladaptive.

7. Show how tactics of impression management may lead to false modesty or self-defeating behavior.

CHAPTER REVIEW

Supply the words necessary to complete each of the following statements.

SELF-CONCEPT: WHO AM I?
1. Our sense of _____ helps organize our thoughts and actions. The self-_____ effect refers to the tendency to remember well information related to oneself. The elements of our self-concept include the specific self-_____ that guide our processing of self-relevant information and the

_____ selves that we dream of or dread. Our self-_____ is our overall self-evaluation.

2. Multiple influences shape the self including the _____ we play, the _____ identity we form, the social _____ we make, our experiences of _____ and _____, other people's _____, and the surrounding _____.

3. Some people, especially in industrialized Western cultures, value _____ (giving priority to one's own goals) and nurture an _____ self. Others, for example in Asian and African cultures, place greater value on _____ (giving priority to the goals of one's group) and nurture an _____ self. These contrasting ideas contribute to cultural differences in social behavior.

4. Factors that have big effects on our behavior we sometimes report as _____ and sometimes perceive factors that have little effect as _____. We also poorly _____ our own future behavior. Studies of perception and memory show that we are more aware of the _____ of our thinking that we are of the thinking _____.

5. We seem to have a _____ attitude system, that is, an automatic _____ attitude and a differing consciously controlled, _____ attitude. People's errors in self-understanding place limits on the scientific usefulness of their _____. Although personal testimonies are powerfully _____, they may also convey unwitting error.

PERCEIVED SELF-CONTROL

6. Bandura formulated the concept of _____, that is, the sense that one is competent and effective. This sense leads us to set challenging _____ and to _____ when facing difficulties. Studies on locus of _____ and learned _____ also indicate that feelings of self-determination facilitate achievement and coping.

SELF-SERVING BIAS

7. When perceiving ourselves we are prone to a potent error: the _____ bias. There is a tendency to blame the _____ for our failures and to accept _____ for our successes. The error is also evident in our tendency to see ourselves as generally "_____ than _____."

8. We demonstrate an unrealistic _____ about future life events. We tend to _____ the commonality of our opinions and _____ the commonality of our abilities.

18

9. Self-serving perceptions arise partly from a motive to maintain and enhance
_____, a motive that protects people from _____ but
which can also contribute to misjudgment and group _____.

SELF-PRESENTATION

10. People sometimes present a different _____ than they feel. The clearest
example is false _____. Sometimes people will even self-
_____ with self-defeating behaviors that protect self-esteem by
providing excuses for _____.

11. _____ refers to our wanting to present a desired image both to other
people and to _____. Those who score high on a scale of
_____ tendency adjust their behavior to create the desired
impression. The tendency to self-present modesty and restrained optimism is particularly
great in cultures that value _____.

MATCHING TERMS

Write the letter of the correct term from the right before the appropriate number on the left

_____ 1. Answer to the question, "Who am I?"

     a. self-efficacy

_____ 2. Images of what we dream of or dread becoming in the future.

     b. self-esteem

     c. self-concept

_____ 3. Beliefs about self that organize and guide the processing of self-relevant information.

     d. self-serving bias

_____ 4. The tendency to overestimate the commonality of one's undesirable behaviors.

     e. possible selves

     f. self-schema

_____ 5. The tendency to remember well information related to oneself.

     g. social identity

_____ 6. Protecting one's self-image with behaviors that create a handy excuse for failure.

     h. false consensus effect

     i. learned helplessness

_____ 7. Is conducive to effective coping and self-improvement.

     j. self-monitoring

_____ 8. Giving priority to one's own goals over group goals.

     k. individualism

_____ 9. May be a by-product of how we process information or a result of a self-esteem motivation.

     l. self-handicapping

     m. false uniqueness effect

     n. self-reference effect

_____ 10. Being attuned to the way one presents oneself in social situations and adjusting one's performance.

_____ 11. The tendency to underestimate the commonality of one's abilities.

_____ 12. The "we" aspect of our self-concept.

_____ 13. Becoming passive and depressed because one's efforts are ineffective.

_____ 14. A person's overall self-evaluation or sense of self-worth.

TRUE-FALSE REVIEW

Circle T if the statement is true and F if it is false.

T F 1. The self-reference effect illustrates how our sense of self is at the center of our worlds.

T F 2. People who took a pill that they thought would produce physical arousal tolerated much more shock than people not given a pill.

T F 3. People are clearly aware of the factors that influence their daily moods.

T F 4. People are much better at predicting their own future behavior than that of others.

T F 5. Studies of perception and memory show that our awareness is mostly of the <u>results</u> of thinking and not of the <u>process</u>.

T F 6. People's expressed attitudes are more likely to predict their behavior if they are first asked to analyze their feelings before indicating their attitudes.

T F 7. Suffering a paralyzing accident affects long-term happiness less than most people suppose.

T F 8. Our "possible selves" include images of the self we fear becoming as well as images of the self we dream of becoming.

T F 9. Japanese are more likely than Americans to complete the statement "I am....." by stating their personal traits or personal goals.

T F 10. When we are feeling securely good about ourselves, we are more likely to berate those who don't like us.

T F 11. On nearly any dimension that is both subjective and socially desirable most people see themselves as better than average.

T F 12. No topic in psychology is today more researched than the self.

T F 13. In the United States, those living in the deep South exhibit greater individualism than do those in Mountain West states such as Oregon and Montana.

T F 14. Mildly depressed people generally see themselves as other people see them.

T F 15. Research indicates that those who exhibit the self-serving bias invariably have low self-esteem.

T F 16. Self-handicapping is typically motivated by feelings of inferiority.

T F 17. According to terror management theory, low self-esteem is adaptive because it buffers death anxiety.

T F 18. The "spotlight effect" demonstrates how collectivists often suffer from low self-esteem.

T F 19. The more physiologically aroused people are after a failure, the more likely they are to excuse the failure with self-protective attributions.

T F 20. If we hold negative ideas about another racial group, we presume that many others also have negative stereotypes.

T F 21. The self-serving bias seems to be restricted to people who live in North America and Europe.

T F 22. People with a strong sense of internal control believe that their destiny is controlled by other people.

T F 23. Martin Seligman maintains that schizophrenia is the result of learned helplessness.

T F 24. People with a strong sense of self-efficacy cope better and achieve more than do people who lack a sense of their own competence and effectiveness.

T F 25. The more that students at English universities identify themselves as British, the less they identify themselves as European.

MULTIPLE-CHOICE PRACTICE TEST

Circle the correct letter.

1. Our perceiving ourselves as athletic, overweight, smart, or shy constitutes our

    a. egocentric beliefs
    b. interdependent self
    c. self-schemas
    d. self-references

2. According to Hazel Markus and her colleagues, our "possible selves"

    a. include our vision of the self we dream of becoming and the self we fear becoming
    b. include only our vision of the self we hope we will become
    c. are the specific self-schemas that determine our self-esteem
    d. are the ideal images that close friends and relatives have of us

3. The tendency to process efficiently and remember well information related to oneself is called the _____ effect.

   a. self-aggrandizing   c. self-processing
   b. self-schematizing   d. self-reference

4. Self-esteem refers to

   a. the sum total of our possible selves
   b. our overall self-evaluation
   c. the sum total of all our thoughts about ourselves
   d. our most central self-schemas

5. When people are asked whether they would comply with demands to deliver cruel shocks or would be hesitant to help a victim if several other people were present,

   a. they overwhelmingly deny their vulnerability to such influences
   b. they admit they might be influenced but in their actual behavior are not
   c. males deny they would be influenced, but females admit they would
   d. they accurately predict their future behavior on such significant matters

6. Research has indicated that when people are asked to record their daily mood and the factors that might influence it,

   a. there is little relationship between their perception of how important a factor was and how well the factor predicted their moods
   b. females have better insight into what affects their moods than do males
   c. people have much better insight into what influences their own moods than what influences the mood of a friend
   d. adults have better insight into what affects their moods than do children

7. Timothy Wilson suggests that the mental processes that _____ our social behavior are distinct from the mental processes through which we _____ our behavior.

   a. control; explain   c. produce; control
   b. evaluate; inhibit   d. form; change

8. In nine experiments, Timothy Wilson and his colleagues found that people's expressed attitudes predicted their later behavior reasonably well <u>unless</u>

   a. their attitudes were inconsistent with social norms
   b. the experimenter had them under surveillance
   c. they were asked to rationally analyze their feelings before indicating their attitudes
   d. they had little opportunity to reflect on their feelings before indicating their attitudes

9. According to the text, research on self-knowledge suggests that

   a. people tend to underestimate their own abilities
   b. people who have an interdependent self show less self-insight than those with an independent self
   c. people are highly accurate in predicting their own future behavior
   d. people's self-reports are often untrustworthy

10. In comparison to people in Western cultures, people in Asian cultures are more likely to demonstrate

   a. learned helplessness   c. self-serving bias
   b. self-handicapping   d. an interdependent self

11. What motto best represents societies that nurture an independent self?

   a. "No one is an island"
   b. "Birds of a feather flock together"
   c. "To thine own self be true"
   d. "One who hesitates is lost"

12. An internal locus of control is to _____ as unrealistic optimism is to _____.

   a. self-presentation; self-serving bias
   b. self-serving bias; fundamental attribution error
   c. self-efficacy; self-serving bias
   d. self-handicapping; self-efficacy

13. Bandura is to _____ as Rotter is to _____.

   a. learned helplessness; self-serving bias
   b. interdependent self; independent self
   c. self-efficacy; locus of control
   d. self-serving bias; fundamental attribution error

14. People who believe themselves internally controlled are more likely to

   a. take unnecessary risks
   b. engage in self-handicapping
   c. be tolerant of racial differences
   d. do well in school

15. Dogs who learn a sense of helplessness by being taught they cannot escape shocks

    a. tend to band together and as a group demonstrate collective efficacy
    b. tend to become highly aggressive in other situations
    c. more readily take the initiative to escape punishment when that becomes possible
    d. later fail to take the initiative in another situation when they can escape punishment

16. The fact that students tend to have a higher academic self-concept if they attend a school with few exceptionally capable students is best explained in terms of

    a. locus of control   c. social comparison
    b. self-handicapping   d. self-monitoring

17. Research findings challenge the notion that

    a. most people suffer from unrealistically low self-esteem
    b. we tend to blame others for their own misfortune
    c. we strive to protect and enhance our self-esteem
    d. true humility consists of self-forgetfulness

18. Charles H. Cooley's concept of the "looking-glass self" recognizes that our self-concept is shaped by

    a. the roles we play
    b. social comparison
    c. success and failure experiences
    d. other people's judgments

19. College students perceive themselves as far more likely than their classmates to _____ and as far less likely to _____

    a. draw a good salary; develop a drinking problem
    b. obtain a divorce; own a home
    c. travel to Europe; be happy in their work
    d. become a mental patient; have close friendships

20. We tend to _____ the commonality of our unsuccessful behaviors and _____ the commonality of our successful behaviors.

    a. overestimate; underestimate   c. underestimate; underestimate
    b. underestimate; overestimate   d. overestimate; overestimate

21. Gang leaders, extreme ethnocentrists, and terrorists tend to have _____ self-esteem.

    a. much lower than average
    b. somewhat lower than average
    c. average
    d. higher than average

22. Research on self-perception indicates that if we find ourselves linked (say born on the same day as) to some reprehensible person

    a. we show a temporary loss of self-esteem
    b. we form a more independent self
    c. we form a harsher view of the person
    d. we soften our view of the person

23. Abraham Tesser has argued that a "_____" motive is important in helping us understand friction among brothers and sisters who share similar abilities.

    a. cognitive dissonance
    b. self-esteem maintenance
    c. self-forgetfulness
    d. social approval maintenance

24. High self-esteem goes hand in hand with

    a. self-serving perceptions
    b. self-monitoring
    c. an independent self
    d. a tendency to berate others

25. According to "terror management theory," positive self-esteem protects us from feeling anxiety over

    a. social rejection
    b. our own death
    c. public speaking
    d. failing to achieve an important goal

26. Those who do not exhibit self-serving bias may tend toward

    a. better than average mental health
    b. schizophrenia
    c. above average intelligence
    d. depression

27. Self-presentation, self-handicapping, and self-monitoring all reflect human efforts at

    a. self-efficacy
    b. self-understanding
    c. collective efficacy
    d. impression management

28. In contrast to those with an independent self-concept, those with an interdependent self-concept are most likely to disapprove

    a. nationalism
    b. risk-taking
    c. conformity
    d. egotism

29. The self-handicapping strategy enables us to

    a. accept greater responsibility for our failures
    b. avoid the fundamental attribution error
    c. take greater credit for our successes
    d. circumvent the ill effects of the Peter Principle

30. Students are more likely to rate themselves as superior in _____ than in _____.

    a. moral goodness; intelligence
    b. being punctual; being disciplined
    c. creativity; honesty
    d. contributing money to the poor; caring for the poor

31. People are more modest when

    a. experts will be scrutinizing their self-evaluations
    b. they have a strong sense of self-efficacy
    c. they present themselves to others they regard as inferior
    d. they present themselves to members of their own family

32. Being attuned to the way one presents oneself in social situations and adjusting one's performance to create the desired impression is called

    a. self-handicapping   c. egocentric role-playing
    b. self-monitoring   d. manipulative social adjustment

33. In completing the statement, "I am...." Michelle responds by stating that she is the youngest in her family, belongs to a sorority, and is a member of the community orchestra. Michelle's statements most clearly reflect

    a. her possible selves   c. a self-serving bias
    b. an interdependent self   d. a strong self-monitoring tendency

34. Because she gets poor grades no matter how hard she studies, Milly has decided not to study at all. Milly's behavior most clearly demonstrates

    a. self-serving bias   c. learned helplessness
    b. unrealistic optimism   d. a self-monitoring tendency

35. Individualism is to _____ as collectivism is to _____.

    a. North American cultures; western European cultures
    b. industrialized Western cultures; Asian cultures
    c. third world cultures; Asian cultures
    d. Mexico; Canada

36. Betsy never plans ahead because she believes that the way things turn out is merely a matter of chance. Betsy's thinking most clearly illustrates

    a. the false uniqueness bias
    b. an external locus of control
    c. self-handicapping
    d. self-efficacy

37. Judging from the discussion of self-image in the text, people are least likely to see themselves as above average in

    a. leadership ability
    b. tolerance
    c. weight
    d. helpfulness

38. Although Jeff frequently exceeds the speed limit by at least 10 miles per hour, he justifies his behavior by erroneously thinking that most other drivers do the same. His mistaken belief best illustrates

    a. learned helplessness
    b. false consensus
    c. self-monitoring
    d. an interdependent self

39. Those who evade paying income tax but who give generously to charity will probably _____ the number of others who evade taxes and _____ the number of others who give generously to charity.

    a. overestimate; overestimate
    b. underestimate; overestimate
    c. overestimate; underestimate
    d. underestimate; underestimate

40. Tomorrow morning Harry Smith has an interview that will determine whether he will be accepted into medical school. Rather than getting a good night's sleep, he is going to an all-night party with his friends. From the material presented in the text, which of the following may best describe Harry's behavior?

    a. Harry unconsciously hopes he is not accepted into medical school
    b. Harry is making the fundamental attribution error
    c. Harry is engaging in self-handicapping
    d. Harry shares with his friends a sense of collective efficacy

SHORT ESSAY QUESTIONS

Answer the following questions in the space provided.

1. Briefly explain what is meant by "self-schemas" and "possible selves."

2. Identify three factors that shape the development of one's self-concept.

3. Discuss research findings regarding the accuracy of our self-knowledge

4. What is self-efficacy? Briefly describe the results of research on this concept.

5. What is the self-serving bias? Describe two lines of research that demonstrate the presence of the error.

6. Explain why people perceive themselves in self-enhancing ways and briefly describe how a self-serving bias can be adaptive as well as maladaptive.

7. Explain how attempts at impression management may lead to false modesty and self handicapping.

ANSWER KEY

Chapter Review

1. self
   reference
   schema
   possible
   esteem

2. roles
   social
   comparisons
   success
   failure
   judgments
   culture

3. individualism
   independent
   collectivism
   interdependent

4. innocuous
   potent
   predict
   results
   process

5. dual
   implicit
   explicit
   self-reports
   persuasive

6. self-efficacy
   goals
   persist
   control
   helplessness

7. self-serving
   situation
   credit
   better
   average

8. optimism
   overestimate
   underestimate

9. self-esteem
   depression
   conflict

10. self
    modesty
    handicap
    failure

11. Self-presentation
    ourselves
    self-monitoring
    self-restraint

Matching Terms

1. c
2. e
3. f
4. h
5. n
6. l
7. a

8. k
9. d
10. j
11. m
12. g
13. i
14. b

True-False Review

1.	T	14.	T
2.	T	15.	F
3.	F	16.	F
4.	F	17.	F
5.	T	18.	F
6.	F	19.	T
7.	T	20.	T
8.	T	21.	F
9.	F	22.	F
10.	F	23.	F
11.	T	24.	T
12.	T	25.	T
13.	F		

Multiple-Choice Practice Test

1.	c	21.	d
2.	a	22.	d
3.	d	23.	b
4.	b	24.	a
5.	a	25.	b
6.	a	26.	d
7.	a	27.	d
8.	c	28.	d
9.	d	29.	c
10.	d	30.	a
11.	c	31.	a
12.	c	32.	b
13.	c	33.	b
14.	d	34.	c
15.	d	35.	b
16.	c	36.	b
17.	a	37.	c
18.	d	38.	b
19.	a	39.	c
20.	a	40.	c

CHAPTER 3

SOCIAL BELIEFS AND JUDGMENTS

CHAPTER OBJECTIVES

After completing your study of this chapter you should be able to:

1. Identify the assumptions, questions, and general findings of attribution theory.

2. Define the fundamental attribution error and explain why it occurs.

3. Show how our preconceptions control our interpretations and memories.

4. Illustrate and explain the overconfidence phenomenon.

5. Describe the representativeness and availability heuristics.

6. Illustrate the illusions of correlation and personal control.

7. Describe how our moods affect our judgments.

8. Describe how our erroneous beliefs may generate their own reality.

CHAPTER REVIEW

Supply the words necessary to complete each of the following statements.

EXPLAINING OTHERS

1. _____ theory analyzes how we explain people's behavior. It suggests we explain others' behavior either in terms of _____ or _____ causes.

2. Edward Jones and Keith Davis noted that we often infer that people's dispositions _____ to their actions. Harold Kelley described how we use information about _____, distinctiveness, and _____

in explaining behavior. Further evidence of the reasonableness of our attributions comes from Norman Anderson's research on _____ integration.

3. The "_____ attribution error" refers to the tendency for observers to underestimate _____ influences and to overestimate _____ influences upon others' behavior.

4. Even when people know they are _____ someone else's behavior, they still underestimate _____ influences.

5. We commit this error when explaining _____ behavior. We often explain our own behavior in terms of the _____ while holding others _____ for their behavior.

6. Why do we make this attributional error? Attribution theorists point out that we have a different _____ when observing than when acting. When we watch another person act, the _____ occupies the center of our attention. When we act, the _____ commands our attention. Perspectives can change with _____ and circumstances. If people are made _____, they attribute more responsibility to themselves.

7. Other explanations have been offered for the fundamental attribution error. For example, our whole Western worldview inclines us to assume that _____, not _____, cause events.

8. Experiments reveal that the attribution error occurs even when we are aware of the _____ forces. The error is fundamental because it colors our _____ in basic and important ways. For example, people's attributions predict their _____ toward the poor and unemployed.

CONSTRUCTING INTERPRETATIONS AND MEMORIES

9. Certain experiments show that people's preconceived notions bias the way they _____ and interpret information they are given. The effect of prior beliefs on social _____ is so great that even _____ evidence may be seen as supporting one's beliefs.

10. Studies indicate that a falsehood is difficult to demolish if people have invented an _____ for it. The belief perseverance phenomenon can be reduced by having people explain the _____. Research also indicates we easily (though unconsciously) revise our _____. We _____ our past attitudes, past behavior, and experiences.

JUDGING OTHERS

11. People tend to be more _____ than correct. For example, about 30 percent of the time, the correct answers lay outside the range they feel _____ percent confident.

12. The overconfidence phenomenon seems partly due to the fact that people are more likely to search for information that _____ their beliefs than for information that does not. Overconfidence can be reduced by giving people prompt _____ on the accuracy of their judgments and by getting them to think of one good reason why their judgments might be _____.

13. We use mental shortcuts called _____ to form impressions, make judgments, and invent explanations. To judge something by intuitively comparing it to our mental representation of a category is to use the _____ heuristic.

14. People are _____ to deduce particular instances from a general truth but are _____ to infer general truth from a vivid instance. If examples are readily _____ in our memory, we presume that the event is commonplace.

15. People also tend to see _____ where none exists. They readily perceive random events as _____ their beliefs.

16. Our tendency to perceive random events as though they were related feeds the illusion that chance events are subject to our _____. Ellen Langer demonstrated the illusion with experiments on _____. The illusion of control may arise as a result of the statistical phenomenon of _____ toward the _____.

17. Our _____ color how we recall and interpret our world. In a _____ mood, we have more depressing thoughts.

SELF-FULFILLING BELIEFS

18. Studies of _____ bias and teacher expectations illustrate the _____ prophecy: the tendency for our expectations to evoke behavior that confirms them.

CONCLUSIONS

19. Our modes of thought are generally _____ and errors are a by-product of our minds' strategies for simplifying complex information.

MATCHING TERMS

Write the letter of the correct term from the right before the appropriate number on the left.

_____	1. Throwing dice softly for low numbers and and hard for high numbers.	a. priming
		b. misinformation effect
_____	2. Clinging to beliefs in spite of contradictory evidence.	c. illusion of control
_____	3. Activating particular associations in memory.	d. regression toward the average
_____	4. Searching for information that confirms one's expectations.	e. counterfactual thinking
		f. availability heuristic
_____	5. Shows how memory is constructive.	
_____	6. The tendency for one's expectations to evoke behavior that confirms the expectations.	g. overconfidence phenomenon
		h. self-fulfilling prophecy
_____	7. It analyzes how we make judgments about people.	i. belief perseverance
_____	8. Perceiving order in random events.	j. illusory correlation
_____	9. High scorers on one exam obtain lower scores on the next exam.	k. attribution theory
		l. fundamental attribution error
_____	10. Imagining what might have happened but didn't.	
_____	11. Presuming, despite contrary odds, that someone belongs to a particular group if resembling a typical member.	m. representativeness heuristic
_____	12. The tendency to overestimate the the accuracy of one's beliefs.	n. confirmation bias
_____	13. The tendency for observers to underestimate situational influences and overestimate dispositional influences.	
_____	14. Judging the likelihood of events in terms of how quickly they come to mind.	

TRUE-FALSE REVIEW

Circle T if the statement is true and F if it is false.

T F   1. Attribution theorists are primarily concerned with how we are influenced by others, particularly by groups.

T F   2. Fritz Heider concluded that people tend to attribute someone's behavior either to stable or to unstable factors.

T F   3. According to the text, we often form judgments of one another in a reasonable manner.

T F   4. Discounting of situational effects in judging another's behavior is called the fundamental attribution error.

T F   5. Harold Kelley suggests that we use information about "correspondence" in judging the causes of another's behavior.

T F   6. We often explain our own behavior in terms of the situation while holding others responsible for their behavior.

T F   7. Presuppositions clearly affect both everyday and scientific thinking.

T F   8. Memory is like a storage chest into which we deposit material. Occasionally something gets lost from the chest, and then we say we have forgotten.

T F   9. Memories are often reconstructions of the past.

T F 10. The Kulechov effect refers to the fact that collectivists are less vulnerable to the fundamental attribution error.

T F 11. About 30 percent of the time, the correct answers lay outside the range about which people feel 98 percent confident.

T F 12. People tend to seek out confirming rather than disconfirming evidence for their beliefs.

T F 13. Providing people with prompt feedback on the accuracy of their judgments reduces the overconfidence phenomenon.

T F 14. Based upon what Americans tell us about their smoking habits, a third of the cigarettes sold are unaccounted.

T F 15. "Regression toward the average" refers to our tendency to be conformist.

T F 16. The hindsight bias explains why people are more afraid of flying than driving.

T F 17. The availability heuristic provides an explanation for the self-fulfilling prophecy.

T F 18. People are slow to deduce particular instances from a general truth but are quick to infer general truth from a vivid instance.

T F 19. People who chose a lottery number for themselves demanded four times as much money for the sale of their lottery ticket than people whose number was assigned by the experimenter.

T F 20. "Regression toward the average" may help to explain why the illusion of control arises.

T F 21. The results of experimenter bias demonstrate the tendency for one's expectations to evoke behavior that confirms the expectations.

T F 22. Cases of blindsight illustrate how people may know more than they know they know

T F 23. Research indicates that children but not adults construct false memories.

T F 24. Simple, efficient thinking strategies that help us simplify and cope with reality are known as schemata.

T F 25. Most published experiments have confirmed that teachers' expectations significantly influence their students' performance.

MULTIPLE-CHOICE PRACTICE TEST

Circle the correct letter.

1. The theory of how we explain others' behavior is known as

   a. impression theory
   b. inferential analysis theory
   c. cognitive dissonance theory
   d. attribution theory

2. According to the theory of correspondent inferences,

   a. we tend to infer that people's intentions and dispositions correspond to their actions
   b. we tend to infer that people's intentions and dispositions correspond to our own intentions and dispositions
   c. we tend to infer that people share the same underlying motives and values
   d. those who have similar values tend to make the same attributions about others

3. For a school debate, Sally has been asked to argue in favor of capital punishment. Research on the fundamental attribution error suggests that observers of Sally's speech will conclude that her arguments

   a. reflect her true attitude on the topic
   b. reflect a tendency to present herself favorably
   c. are weak because she was assigned to present a particular position on the topic
   d. will lead her to experience cognitive dissonance

4. The tendency for observers to underestimate the impact of the situation and overestimate the impact of inner dispositions upon another's behavior is called

   a. the self-serving bias   c. the fundamental attribution error
   b. the false consensus bias   d. cognitive conceit

5. Evidence of the reasonable manner in which we form judgments of one another comes from research on

   a. informational influence   c. the mere-exposure effect
   b. personal space   d. information integration

6. When subjects were told that a clinical psychology graduate student had been instructed to act in a friendly manner or in an aloof, critical manner, they judged that

   a. the graduate student's aloof manner reflected her personality, but the friendly behavior was due to the situation
   b. both the friendly and aloof behaviors had a situational cause
   c. both the friendly and aloof behaviors reflected the student's true dispositions
   d. the aloof behavior was due to the situation but the friendly behavior reflected her true disposition

7. People from collectivist cultures are more likely than Americans to

   a. offer situational explanations for someone's actions
   b. offer dispositional explanations for someone's actions
   c. engage in self-handicapping
   d. offer self-serving explanations for their own behavior

8. There is a tendency to attribute the causes of _____ behavior to the situation and to attribute the causes of _____ behavior to traits.

   a. our own; others'   c. children's; adults'
   b. others'; our own   d. males'; females'

9. Our tendency to attribute others' behavior to their personal characteristics is reduced when we

    a. view a videotape of the behavior recorded from their perspective
    b. make judgments about criminal behavior
    c. are high in self-efficacy
    d. make judgments about academic performance

10. According to Harold Kelley's theory of attributions, the three factors that influence whether we attribute someone's behavior to internal or external causes are

    a. distinctiveness, consensus, relevance
    b. distinctiveness, consensus, consistency
    c. relevance, consistency, consensus
    d. distinctiveness, consistency, relevance

11. According to the text, the fundamental attribution error may lead us to

    a. overestimate the brilliance of our teachers
    b. fail to hold people responsible for their misconduct
    c. be lenient with convicted criminals
    d. underestimate our own compassion

12. People who were shown the random mix of results from a 50-day cloud-seeding experiment made judgments that showed

    a. an illusory correlation   c. the misinformation effect
    b. the base-rate fallacy   d. counterfactual thinking

13. Women's friendliness is especially likely to be misread as a sexual come-on by men who

    a. have no sisters   c. have low self-esteem
    b. are in positions of power   d. have liberal political attitudes

14. In Olympic competition, _____ medalists exhibit more joy than _____ medalists

    a. bronze; silver   c. bronze; gold
    b. silver; bronze   d. silver; gold

15. In a series of experiments, Elizabeth Loftus has had people witness an effect, receive misleading information about it, and then take a memory test. The repeated finding is

    a. the misinformation effect   c. confirmation bias
    b. counterfactual thinking   d. information integration

16. The more closely we examine our theories and explain how they might be true,

    a. the more uncertain we become of them
    b. the more closed we become to discrediting information
    c. the more open we are likely to become to discrediting information
    d. the more complex our theories are likely to become

17. The tendency of people to cling to their ideas even in the face of contrary evidence is called the

    a. belief perseverance phenomenon   c. belief assimilation phenomenon
    b. availability heuristic   d. denial paradox

18. The Kulechov effect in which people perceive different emotions in an actor's face illustrates

    a. the availability heuristic
    b. memory construction
    c. our use of useless information
    d. how preconceptions control our interpretations

19. The tendency of people to cling to their ideas even in the face of contrary evidence can be reduced by having them

    a. study the hindsight bias
    b. study the evidence more carefully
    c. participate in a debate
    d. explain why the opposite idea might be true

20. In recalling a scene from our past experience we often see ourselves in the scene. This illustrates how

    a. memory is a reconstruction of the past
    b. memory always involves mental imagery
    c. personal memories are often precise copies of the past
    d. memory is heuristic

21. Cases of blindsight as well as prosopagnosia patients demonstrate how

    a. thinking is partly automatic
    b. memory is reconstructive
    c. preconceptions shape interpretations
    d. beliefs can be self-fulfilling

22. When writer Chuck Ross mailed a typewritten copy of Jerzy Kosinski's novel to 28 publishers and literary agencies to consider for publication,

    a. he was accused of plagiarism
    b. most did not recognize it and wanted to publish it
    c. all rejected it including the original publisher
    d. all but the original publisher rejected it

23. Giving people immediate feedback on the accuracy of their judgments

    a. reduces the overconfidence bias
    b. shows no effect on the overconfidence bias
    c. reduces overconfidence bias in children but not in adults
    d. undermines their self-confidence and leads them to make worse errors in judgment

24. Research indicates that participants in self-improvement programs show _____ improvement on average and claim they received _____ improvement.

    a. considerable; modest   c. modest; modest
    b. modest; considerable   d. considerable; considerable

25. The incorrect belief that the letter "k" appears more often as the first letter of a word than as the third letter can be understood in terms of

    a. the availability heuristic   c. regression toward the average
    b. hindsight bias   d. the illusion of control

26. After a 1990 football game between Alabama and Auburn, victorious Alabama fans viewed _____ than did the losing Auburn fans.

    a. war as more likely and advantageous to the United States
    b. war as less likely and potentially devastating
    c. a college degree as less necessary and enriching
    d. a college degree as more valuable and enriching

27. Tversky and Kahneman have identified _____ as a possible cause of the illusion of control.

    a. schemata   c. self-fulfilling prophecy
    b. base-rate fallacy   d. regression toward the average

28. Studies of experimenter bias and teacher expectations have revealed the presence of

    a. hindsight bias   c. self-fulfilling prophecy
    b. illusory correlation   d. a fundamental attribution error

29. Nisbett and Ross believe that education could reduce our vulnerability to errors in social thinking and should include

    a. teaching useful slogans such as "It's an empirical question"
    b. teaching that is illustrated with vivid anecdotes and examples
    c. statistics courses that are geared to everyday problems of logic
    d. all of the above

30. The textbook states that a large drop in prices on the stock market sometimes illustrates

    a. the representativeness heuristic
    b. the availability heuristic
    c. the overconfidence phenomenon
    d. self-fulfilling prophecy

31. You notice that Mary has missed class, and you commit the fundamental attribution error by thinking,

    a. Mary has been required to work overtime
    b. Mary is lazy
    c. Mary's friends stopped by her room unexpectedly
    d. Mary has the flu

32. As a result of making the fundamental attribution error you might be likely to favor

    a. increases in unemployment benefits
    b. increases in international aid to poor countries
    c. more severe penalties for criminal offenses
    d. victim compensation laws

33. Although Fred was certain he answered at least 50 items correctly on his history test, he actually was right on only 40 items. Fred's misjudgment illustrates

    a. the self-fulfilling prophecy
    b. the hindsight bias
    c. the overconfidence phenomenon
    d. regression toward the average

34. Linda is 31, single, and outspoken. As a college student she was deeply concerned with discrimination and other social issues. A tendency to conclude that it is more likely that Linda is a bank teller and active in the feminist movement than simply a bank teller illustrates the powerful influence of

    a. belief perseverance
    b. the availability heuristic
    c. regression toward the average
    d. the representativeness heuristic

35. Despite reading solid research evidence that cigarette smoking causes cancer, Philip continues to believe that smoking is harmless. Philip's thinking clearly reveals

   a. belief assimilation
   b. belief consolidation
   c. belief perseverance
   d. operation of the availability heuristic

36. Many people firmly believe in astrology's ability to predict the future. Assuming they are presented a history of an astrologer's past predictions, which in actuality show a random mix of success and failure, they are likely to

   a. believe the astrologer is successful
   b. question this astrologer's predictive ability but still believe in the validity of astrology
   c. become very defensive
   d. give up their belief in the validity of astrology

37. Bob, a baseball player, makes five hits while Joe, a member of the same team, makes none in a particular game. In the next game, both obtain one hit. What term used in the text explains Bob's fewer hits and Joe's increase?

   a. overconfidence bias
   b. priming
   c. regression to the average
   d. schemata

38. What psychological term might best be used to describe the rule "I before E except after C"?

   a. base-rate fallacy
   b. hindsight bias
   c. illusion of control
   d. heuristic

39. A person enters a casino and after inserting one silver dollar in a slot machine hits the jackpot. This person's tendency to continue putting money into the machine so that finally the amount lost exceeds the original winnings can perhaps best be explained in terms of

   a. self-fulfilling prophecy
   b. regression toward the average
   c. illusion of control
   d. hindsight bias

40. The people in a small town become convinced that the bank where they have their savings accounts is unsound. The next day, most of them demand their savings. By the end of the day, the bank is unable to pay off all those who want their deposits. This is an example of

   a. regression toward the average
   b. self-fulfilling prophecy
   c. the hindsight bias
   d. illusory correlation

SHORT ESSAY QUESTIONS

Answer the following questions in the space provided.

1. Briefly describe the central concern of attribution theory. According to Fritz Heider, to what two kinds of causes do we attribute behavior?

2. What is the fundamental attribution error? Why does it occur?

3. Describe what is meant by the term "memory construction."

4. Give one reason why we are overconfident.

5. Distinguish between the availability heuristic and the representativeness heuristic.

6. Provide one example of illusory correlation and one example of the illusion of control

7. Discuss the implications of self-fulfilling prophecy for the classroom

Chapter Review

1. Attribution
   internal
   external

2. correspond
   consistency
   consensus
   information

3. fundamental
   situational
   dispositional

4. causing
   external

5. others'
   situation
   responsible

6. perspective
   person
   environment
   time
   self-conscious

7. people
   situations

8. situational
   explanations
   attitudes

9. perceive
   perception
   contradictory

10. explanation
    opposite
    memories
    reconstruct

11. confident
    98

12. confirms
    feedback
    wrong

13. heuristics
    representativeness

14. slow
    quick
    available

15. correlation
    confirming

16. influence
    gambling
    regression
    average

17. moods
    bad

18. experimenter
    self-fulfilling

19. adaptive

Matching Terms

1.	c	8.	j
2.	i	9.	d
3.	a	10.	e
4.	n	11.	m
5.	b	12.	g
6.	h,	13.	l
7.	k	14.	f

True-False Review

1.	F	14.	T
2.	F	15.	F
3.	T	16.	F
4.	T	17.	F
5.	F	18.	T
6.	T	19.	T
7.	T	20.	T
8.	F	21.	T
9.	T	22.	T
10.	T	23.	F
11.	T	24.	F
12.	T	25.	F
13.	T		

Multiple-Choice Practice Test

1.	d	21.	a
2.	a	22.	c
3.	a	23.	a
4.	c	24.	b
5.	d	25.	a
6.	c	26.	b
7.	a	27.	d
8.	a	28.	c
9.	a	29.	d
10.	b	30.	d
11.	a	31.	b
12.	a	32.	c
13.	b	33.	c
14.	a	34.	d
15.	a	35.	c
16.	b	36.	a
17.	a	37.	c
18.	d	38.	d
19.	d	39.	c
20.	a	40.	b

CHAPTER 4

BEHAVIOR AND ATTITUDES

<u>CHAPTER OBJECTIVES</u>

After completing your study of this chapter you should be able to:

1. Identify the components of an attitude.

2. Describe research findings on the relationship between attitudes and behavior.

3. Identify the conditions under which attitudes predict behavior.

4. Provide evidence that behavior determines attitudes.

5. Give three explanations for why our actions affect our attitudes.

6. Describe how rewards influence attitudes.

<u>CHAPTER REVIEW</u>

Supply the words necessary to complete each of the following statements.

1. An attitude is a favorable or unfavorable _____ reaction toward something or someone, exhibited in one's _____, feelings, or intended _____.

DO ATTITUDES DETERMINE BEHAVIOR?

2. During the 1960s research findings led social psychologists to question whether _____ determine _____. At about the same time, personality psychologists began to suspect that personality _____ also fail to predict _____. As a result, the developing picture of what controls our behavior seemed to focus on _____ factors.

3. Social psychologists never get a direct reading on people's attitudes. Instead they measure _____ attitudes, which like other behaviors, are subject to _____ influences. Jones and Sigall invented the bogus _____, which is a procedure for detecting people's true attitudes.

4. Attitudes predict behavior when other _____ upon our behavior are minimal, when the attitude is specifically _____ to the observed behavior, and when the attitude is _____. Making people _____ promotes consistency between words and deeds. Attitudes forged through _____ are more likely to guide actions.

DOES BEHAVIOR DETERMINE ATTITUDES?

5. An important lesson recent social psychology teaches is that we are likely not only to _____ ourselves into a way of acting but also to _____ ourselves into a way of thinking.

6. For example, the actions prescribed by a social _____ readily mold a person's attitudes. People come to believe what they _____, provided they are not bribed or coerced into doing so. Research on the _____ phenomenon indicates that performing a small act (for example, agreeing to do a small favor) later makes people more willing to do a larger one.

7. _____ acts corrode one's conscience, and oppressors frequently _____ their victims. Fortunately the principle works in the other direction as well. _____ action strengthens one's conscience.

8. More positive interracial behavior may lead to the reduction of racial _____. Brainwashing includes a gradual _____ of demands and active _____ in an attempt to change a person's loyalties.

WHY DO ACTIONS AFFECT ATTITUDES?

9. _____ theory assumes that people express attitudes in line with their _____ to create a good impression.

10. Cognitive _____ theory states that people are motivated to justify their behavior after acting contrary to their attitudes or after making a difficult _____. The theory further proposes that the less _____ justification we have for an undesirable action the more we will feel _____ for it and thus the more _____ is aroused and the more our attitudes change.

11. _____ theory assumes that when we are _____ of our attitudes we simply observe our _____ and its

circumstances and infer what our attitudes must be. An important implication of this theory is the _____ effect: Rewarding people to do what they like doing anyway turns their pleasure into work.

12. Dissonance theory explains attitude _____ while self-perception theory explains attitude _____.

MATCHING TERMS

Write the letter of the correct term from the right before the appropriate number on the left

_____ 1. Participants showed a growing confusion between role-playing and self-identity.

_____ 2. The tendency for people who have first agreed to a small request to comply later with a larger request.

_____ 3. A consequence of bribing people to do what they already like doing.

_____ 4. Actions expected of those who occupy a particular social position.

_____ 5. Includes beliefs, feelings, and behavior tendencies.

_____ 6. Reduction of dissonance by internally justifying one's behavior when external inducements do not fully justify it.

_____ 7. Uses principle of active participation to shape thought.

_____ 8. Presumably uses miniature muscular responses to measure attitudes.

_____ 9. A technique for getting people to agree to do something.

_____ 10. Expressing oneself and behaving in ways designed to create a favorable impression or an impression that corresponds to one's ideals.

_____ 11. When we are unsure of our attitudes we infer them by examining our behavior.

_____ 12. Tension that results when two beliefs are inconsistent.

a. attitude

b. bogus pipeline

c. foot-in-the door phenomenon

d. low-ball technique

e. cognitive dissonance

f. self-presentation theory

g. insufficient justification effect

h. self-perception theory

i. overjustification effect

j. brainwashing

k. Stanford Prison simulation

l. role

TRUE-FALSE REVIEW

Circle T if the statement is true and F if it is false.

T F 1. An attitude is composed of beliefs, feelings, and inclinations to act.

T F 2. Allan Wicker reported that the expressed attitudes of a group of people predict about 90 percent of the variations in their behaviors.

T F 3. People's expressed religious attitudes show no relationship to the total quantity of their religious behaviors over a period of time.

T F 4. The bogus pipeline is a brainwashing technique.

T F 5. Attitudes toward contraception strongly predict contraceptive use.

T F 6. People's expressed attitudes predict their average behavior much better than their behavior in a specific situation.

T F 7. Daniel Batson and his colleagues found that the use of mirrors brings behavior in line with espoused moral attitudes.

T F 8. Guards and prisoners in the Stanford prison simulation quickly absorbed the roles they played.

T F 9. Appeals for safe driving habits have had less effect on accident rates than have lower speed limits and divided highways.

T F 10. Experiments indicate that positive behavior toward someone fosters liking for that person.

T F 11. "Low-balling" is an example of the overjustification effect.

T F 12. The low-ball technique has proven to be ineffective because it assumes attitudes determine behavior.

T F 13. Research indicates that if people have granted a small request they are more likely to refuse to grant a larger request that comes later.

T F 14. Severe threats tend to be more effective than mild threats in getting children to internalize a moral principle.

T F 15. Research on racial attitudes and behavior suggests that to change racial behavior one must first change racial attitudes.

T F 16. A gradual escalation of demands and active participation are both components of effective brainwashing.

T F 17. Faculty members write more glowing letters of recommendation to graduate school when students reserve the right to inspect them.

T F 18. Voters indicate more confidence in their candidate just after voting than just before voting.

T F 19. Dissonance theory predicts that when there is external justification for performing an act, dissonance will be high.

T F 20. Self-perception theory assumes that we infer our own attitudes by looking at our behavior.

T F 21. Dissonance is likely to occur after making an important and difficult decision.

T F 22. The greater the reward promised for an activity, the more one will come to enjoy the activity.

T F 23. Japanese people are less likely to exhibit the behavior rationalization commonly found in dissonance experiments.

T F 24. Research indicates that alcohol can provide a substitute way to reduce dissonance.

T F 25. Cognitive dissonance theory provides a better explanation for the overjustification effect than does self-perception theory.

MULTIPLE-CHOICE PRACTICE TEST

Circle the correct letter.

1. The "ABC's of attitudes" refers to

   a. aptitudes, brainwashing, and cognition
   b. attraction, behavior, and compliance
   c. affect, behavior, and cognition
   d. affect, bogus pipeline, and cognitive dissonance

2. In 1971, social psychologist Allan Wicker said, "It may be desirable to abandon the attitude concept." Wicker made this statement because

   a. no one could provide an adequate measure of attitudes
   b. attitudes did not seem to have much effect on behavior
   c. social psychologists could not agree on a definition of an attitude
   d. the study of attitudes had obscured the study of other influences on behavior

3. Which of the following is a technique for measuring attitudes?

   a. self-monitoring pipeline   c. low-ball technique
   b. foot-in-the-door phenomenon   d. bogus pipeline

4. Regan and Fazio found that while all Cornell students expressed a negative attitude toward a housing shortage which had some students sleeping in the dormitory lounges, only _____ acted on their attitudes.

   a. self-monitoring students
   b. those with mirrors in their rooms
   c. those whose attitudes were rooted in direct experience with the temporary housing
   d. those who were former members of a radical social movement

5. Based on recent social-psychological research, which of the following statements is true?

   a. our attitudes and our behavior are unrelated
   b. our attitudes determine our behavior, but our behavior does not determine our attitudes
   c. our behavior determines our attitudes, but our attitudes do not determine our behavior
   d. under certain circumstances attitudes do predict behavior

6. Daniel Batson and his colleagues found that when research participants could assign themselves or someone else to an appealing versus a dull task, most

   a. felt that assigning themselves to the appealing task was the moral thing to do
   b. assigned themselves to the appealing task
   c. asked someone else to make the assignment
   d. made the assignment on the basis of a coin flip

7. Research suggests that to change health habits through persuasion, we should alter people's attitudes toward

   a. specific health practices
   b. the general concept of "health fitness"
   c. health authorities
   d. the value of life itself

8. According to the text, our attitudes will predict our behavior if

   a. we are made aware of social norms
   b. the attitudes are unrelated to central values
   c. as we act, we are conscious of our attitudes
   d. we feel anxious or insecure

9. Rewards and praise that inform people of their achievements _____ intrinsic motivation. Rewards that seek to control people _____ intrinsic motivation.

   a. strengthen; strengthen
   b. weaken; strengthen
   c. strengthen; weaken
   d. weaken; weaken

10. John Cacioppo and his colleagues found that people provided more positive ratings of Chinese characters when

   a. pressing their arms upward
   b. sticking out their tongues
   c. moving their heads left to right
   d. drinking strong coffee

11. Researchers found that after complying with a request to display a 3-inch "Be a safe driver" sign, Californians were

   a. more likely to obey traffic laws
   b. more likely to break the speed limit
   c. less likely to comply later with a request to place a large, ugly "Drive Carefully" sign in their front yards
   d. more likely to comply later with a request to place a large, ugly "Drive Carefully" sign in their front yards

12. The tendency for oppressors to disparage their victims is given in the text as an example of

   a. how attitudes determine behavior
   b. how behavior determines attitudes
   c. the low-balling effect
   d. how role playing comes to shape one's self-identity

13. Which of the following is cited in the text as an example of how changing behavior can alter attitudes?

   a. civil rights legislation
   b. prohibition
   c. traffic laws
   d. capital punishment legislation

14. To prevent customers from canceling their purchases, encyclopedia salespeople may

    a. have the customer fill out the sales agreement
    b. make a second call to the customer three days after the sale
    c. attempt to sell a second more expensive item to the customer
    d. recruit the customer to be an encyclopedia salesperson

15. The theory that states that we adopt certain attitudes in order to justify our past actions is _____ theory.

    a. cognitive dissonance   c. self-perception
    b. self-presentation   d. psychological reactance

16. Research has indicated that racetrack bettors who have just placed their bets are

    a. more optimistic about their bet than those who are about to bet
    b. less confident about their bet than those who are about to bet
    c. less enthusiastic about the sport of horse racing than those who are about to bet
    d. more susceptible to persuasive attempts than those who are about to bet

17. Which of the following is not given in the text as an example of how behavior shapes attitudes?

    a. brainwashing of American POWs
    b. children's resistance to temptation
    c. the German greeting of "Heil Hitler"
    d. the bogus-pipeline effect

18. The gradual escalation of demands and active participation were described as key elements in

    a. the overjustification effect   c. the underjustification effect
    b. brainwashing   d. the low-balling effect

19. Which of the following theories suggests that people express attitudes in line with how they acted in order to avoid looking foolishly inconsistent?

    a. cognitive dissonance theory   c. self-presentation theory
    b. self-perception theory   d. role-playing theory

20. According to the text, we are least likely to feel dissonance when we

    a. have made a difficult decision
    b. do not feel responsible for our behavior
    c. have harmed a friend
    d. have been paid a small sum of money for telling a lie

21. The author of cognitive dissonance theory was

   a. Wicker
   b. Bem
   c. Festinger
   d. Bandura

22. According to self-perception theory, behavior shapes attitudes

   a. only of self-monitoring people
   b. when behavior is inconsistent with attitudes
   c. when attitudes are weak and ambiguous
   d. only in the area of politics and religion

23. When severe and mild threats were used in an attempt to prevent children from engaging in a prohibited activity,

   a. only the severe threat was strong enough to deter the children from engaging in the prohibited activity
   b. both threats deterred the children, but those given the mild threat showed greater internalization of the rule
   c. both threats deterred the children, but those given the severe threat showed greater internalization of the rule
   d. neither threat was successful in getting the children to internalize the rule

24. College students experienced more empathy for a victim receiving electric shock when they were t

   a. something about the victim's life history
   b. that the victim would later be compensated for receiving the shock
   c. that the victim would later reverse roles with the person delivering the shock
   d. to imitate the victim's expression of pain

25. Both cognitive dissonance theory and self-perception theory provide an explanation for the

   a. hindsight bias
   b. insufficient justification effect
   c. overjustification effect
   d. self-monitoring tendency

26. According to self-perception theory, rewards do not diminish intrinsic interest if

   a. the rewards are unanticipated
   b. the rewards are large
   c. the rewards are small
   d. social approval accompanies any monetary reward

27. The theory that best explains the overjustification effect is

    a. cognitive dissonance theory   c. self-perception theory
    b. self-presentation theory   d. aggregation theory

28. Students who had been induced to write an essay favoring a big tuition increase reduced their dissonance by adjusting their attitudes unless

    a. after writing the essay they drank alcohol
    b. they were related to the administrators at the college
    c. they were college seniors
    d. they were self-monitoring persons

29. According to the text, which of the following is true of self-perception and cognitive dissonance theories?

    a. self-perception theory has significantly more support than cognitive dissonance theory
    b. cognitive dissonance theory has been proven correct, and self-perception theory is still being tested
    c. they are contradictory theories; therefore both cannot have validity
    d. evidence exists to support both theories, suggesting wisdom in both

30. Self-perception theory is to _____ as dissonance theory is to _____.

    a. attitude formation; attitude change
    b. attitude change; attitude formation
    c. impression formation; self-monitoring
    d. self-monitoring; impression formation

31. According to Claude Steele, people are aroused by their dissonant behavior because it often

    a. leads to physical punishment
    b. challenges their sense of purpose or meaning in life
    c. threatens their sense of self-worth
    d. leads to social rejection

32. Which of the following is a component of Mary's attitude toward smoking?

    a. Mary believes smoking is harmful to one's health
    b. Mary dislikes the fact that people are permitted to smoke in vehicles of public transportation
    c. Mary is actively working for legislation which would outlaw the sale of cigarettes
    d. all of the above are part of Mary's attitude toward smoking

33. A car salesman offers to sell a customer a new car for $17,000, which is a very attractive price. After the customer signs the papers to purchase at that price, the salesman seeks final approval from the manager. He returns to tell the customer that the manager will sell the car for $17,700. The customer still agrees to buy. The customer was a victim of

a. the overjustification effect   c. brainwashing
b. low-balling   d. the door-in-the-face phenomenon

34. Rhonda is more successful in getting her fellow students to donate blood if they have first agreed to having a bumper sticker advertising the campus blood drive placed on their car. Rhonda's strategy illustrates the

a. overjustification effect   c. low-ball technique
b. foot-in-the-door phenomenon   d. underjustification effect

35. Nicole loses her former interest in playing the piano after her father promises to pay her two dollars for each hour of practice. This illustrates the _____ effect.

a. insufficient justification   c. overjustification
b. low-ball   d. door-in-the-face

36. Although John is strongly opposed to stricter parking regulations on campus, he is asked to write a paper supporting them. Dissonance theory predicts that his attitude will undergo the most change if he

a. refuses to write the paper
b. agrees to write the paper for $200
c. agrees to write the paper for no pay
d. refuses to write the paper even after being offered $20

37. Milford has always strongly believed that it is wrong to cheat. But after he himself cheats on a chemistry quiz, his attitude toward cheating becomes significantly less harsh. What best accounts for this attitude shift?

a. cognitive dissonance theory   c. reinforcement theory
b. self-perception theory   d. role-playing theory

38. Jennifer had great difficulty deciding whether to attend a local community college or the state university. She finally decided to attend the community college. Dissonance theory predicts that her evaluation of the community college is likely to become more _____ and her evaluation of the state university is likely to become more _____.

a. positive; positive   c. negative; positive
b. positive; negative   d. negative; negative

39. In which of the following situations would cognitive dissonance theorists predict that the person is experiencing dissonance?

    a. Dan is trying to decide whether to buy a new or used bicycle
    b. just as Mike finishes mowing the lawn, it begins to rain
    c. Sara has just been accepted into law school
    d. Nancy has just chosen to attend City College rather than State University after receiving equally attractive scholarship offers from both

40. "Let me see, do I like Chinese food? I guess I do because I eat at a Chinese restaurant twice a month." The process reflected in this internal dialogue is best understood in terms of

    a. cognitive dissonance theory
    b. self-perception theory
    c. reinforcement theory
    d. equity theory

SHORT ESSAY QUESTIONS

Answer the following questions in the space provided.

1. Briefly describe the major components of an attitude.

2. What research findings led social and personality psychologists in the 1960s to emphasize the importance of external social influences on behavior?

3. Identify three conditions under which attitudes are likely to predict behavior.

4. List four lines of evidence that indicate behavior affects attitude.

5. How does self-presentation theory explain the effect of our actions on our attitude reports?

6. Briefly compare and contrast self-perception theory and cognitive dissonance theory

7. Explain the insufficient justification effect and the overjustification effect.

ANSWER KEY

Chapter Review

1. evaluative
   beliefs
   behavior

2. attitudes
   behavior
   traits
   behavior
   external

3. expressed
   outside
   pipeline

4. influences
   relevant
   potent
   self-aware
   experience

5. think
   act

6. role
   say
   foot-in-the-door

7. Cruel
   disparage
   Moral

8. prejudice
   escalation
   participation

9. Self-presentation
   actions

10. dissonance
    decision
    external
    responsible
    dissonance

11. Self-perception
    unsure
    behavior
    overjustification

12. change
    formation

Matching Terms

1. k
2. c
3. i
4. l
5. a
6. g
7. j
8. b
9. d
10. f
11. h
12. e

True-False Review

1.	T	14.	F
2.	F	15.	F
3.	F	16.	T
4.	F	17.	T
5.	T	18.	T
6.	T	19.	F
7.	T	20.	T
8.	T	21.	T
9.	T	22.	F
10.	T	23.	T
11.	F	24.	T
12.	F	25.	F
13.	F		

Multiple-Choice Practice Test

1.	c	21.	c
2.	b	22.	c
3.	d	23.	b
4.	c	24.	d
5.	d	25.	b
6.	b	26.	a
7.	a	27.	c
8.	c	28.	a
9.	c	29.	d
10.	a	30.	a
11.	d	31.	c
12.	b	32.	d
13.	a	33.	b
14.	a	34.	b
15.	a	35.	c
16.	a	36.	c
17.	d	37.	a
18.	b	38.	b
19.	c	39.	d
20.	b	40.	b

CHAPTER 5

GENES, CULTURE, AND GENDER

<u>CHAPTER OBJECTIVES</u>

After completing your study of this chapter you should be able to:

1. Identify two important perspectives on human similarities and differences.

2. Describe the major themes of evolutionary psychology.

3. Discuss the nature and function of norms.

4. Identify some differing cultural norms and at least one universal norm.

5. Describe the nature of roles and the various effects of role playing.

6. Discuss important gender similarities and differences.

7. Explain how the evolutionary psychologist accounts for gender differences and describe how hormonal differences predispose psychological differences.

8. Discuss how gender roles vary with culture and over time.

9. Describe the relationship between biology and culture, and discuss the "great lesson" of social psychology.

<u>CHAPTER REVIEW</u>

Supply the words necessary to complete each of the following statements.

HUMAN NATURE AND CULTURAL DIVERSITY

1. Social _____ has become the explosive problem of our time. Two

   perspectives dominate current thinking on human _____ and

_____. The _____ perspective emphasizes human kinship and the _____ perspective emphasizes human diversity.

2. Evolutionary psychologists study how _____ selection favors psychological traits that enhance the preservation and spread of one's _____. The evolutionary perspective highlights our _____ human nature.

3. Perhaps our most important similarity, the hallmark of our species, is our capacity to _____ and to adapt. It enables those in one _____ to value promptness and frankness while those in another do not.

4. All cultures have their own norms, or _____ for accepted and expected behavior. Norms restrain and control but they also _____ the social machinery so that our words and acts come effortlessly. Cultures vary in their norms for expressiveness and _____ space. For reasons unknown, cultures near the equator prefer _____ space, and more touching and hugging.

5. Although cultural norms vary greatly, Roger Brown has described one _____ norm, which concerns how people of unequal _____ relate to one another. We communicate informally with intimates and those of _____ status, and formally with strangers and those of _____ status. Increased _____ is usually initiated by the person with higher status.

6. A role is a set of _____ associated with a given social position. People assigned a _____ status come to see themselves as meriting favorable treatment. Likewise, playing a _____ role can have demeaning effects. However, role-playing can also be used constructively. Through role _____ we can develop empathy for another.

GENDER SIMILARITIES AND DIFFERENCES

7. In childhood, _____ strive for independence while _____ value connectedness. Adult relationships extend this difference. In conversation, men more often than women focus on _____, while women focus on personal _____. Women are more likely to describe themselves as having _____ and tend to be better at reading others' _____.

8. In essentially every society, men are socially _____. Research indicates that men also exhibit more physical _____. There is also a gender gap in _____ attitudes and assertiveness.

EVOLUTION AND GENDER: DOING WHAT COMES NATURALLY?

9. Evolutionary psychologists maintain that natural selection explains males' greater physical _____ and _____ initiative. Men everywhere are attracted

72

to women whose physical features suggest _____. Everywhere, women prefer men with resources and _____. The gender gap in aggression does seem influenced by the sex hormone _____. Hormonal changes provide one explanation for why gender differences _____ with age

CULTURE AND GENDER

10. Behavior _____ for males and females define gender roles. The impact of _____ on gender roles is enormous and is evident from the striking _____ in gender roles throughout the world and across _____. Much of this influence is transmitted via _____.

CONCLUSIONS

11. _____ and _____ explanations need not be contradictory. What biology initiates, culture may _____. They also _____ with one another.

12. Power resides in both persons and situations. They _____ in at least three ways. First, individuals vary in how they interpret and _____ to a given situation. Second, people _____ many of the situations that influence them. Third, people help _____ their social situations.

MATCHING TERMS

Write the letter of the correct term from the right before the appropriate number on the left.

_____ 1. Important vehicle of cultural influence.

_____ 2. A set of behavior expectations for males or females.

_____ 3. Putting oneself in another's shoes.

_____ 4. Natural selection and cultural selection working together.

_____ 5. They prescribe proper behavior.

_____ 6. The taboo against incest.

_____ 7. Identified a universal norm.

_____ 8. Capable of both assertiveness and nurturance.

_____ 9. The relationship between persons and situations.

_____ 10. Can produce empathy for others.

_____ 11. Social behaviors are subject to natural selection.

_____ 12. Behavior intended to hurt someone.

_____ 13. Characteristics by which people define male and female.

_____ 14. Its size depends upon our familiarity with whomever is near us.

a. Brown

b. empathy

c. aggression

d. coevolution

e. androgynous

f. a universal norm

g. gender role

h. evolutionary psychology

i. role reversal

j. gender

k. peers

l. interaction

m. norms

n. personal space

74

TRUE-FALSE REVIEW

Circle T if the statement is true and F if it is false.

T F 1. An evolutionary perspective tends to emphasize our human kinship rather than our diversity.

T F 2. Most people rate their feelings regarding "women" as more favorable than their feelings regarding "men."

T F 3. The portable bubble that we like to maintain between ourselves and others is called a cognitive map.

T F 4. Brown's universal norm is primarily concerned with the way males and females relate to each other.

T F 5. The taboo against incest is a universal norm.

T F 6. A role is defined by a whole cluster of norms.

T F 7. All societies rank people by authority and status.

T F 8. Coevolution is really just another term for role reversal.

T F 9. Role-playing is always destructive to interpersonal relationships.

T F 10. Among our universal similarities, the hallmark of our species is our capacity to learn and to adapt.

T F 11. Worldwide, men are roughly 20 times more likely to murder men than women are to murder women.

T F 12. Males and females show no differences in sexual attitudes.

T F 13. Women tend to be better at reading others' emotions.

T F 14. Across cultures, men tend to marry younger women.

T F 15. National Football League players have higher than normal testosterone levels.

T F 16. In conversation, men tend to interrupt more than do women.

T F 17. Across cultures, males and females are equally likely to initiate sexual relations.

T F 18. Two children in the same family are on average as different from one another as are pairs of children selected randomly from the population.

T F 19. The term "gender role" refers to one's feeling of being a male or female.

T F 20. Compared to boys, girls are much less likely to suffer hyperactivity or speech disorders.

T F 21. Research suggests that marital happiness is highest when both husband and wife have traditionally feminine qualities.

T F 22. In many cultures, boys spend as much time as girls helping with housework and child care.

T F 23. In comparison to men, women describe themselves in more relational terms and are more attuned to others' relationships.

T F 24. Studies indicate that as men and women grow older, they become more androgynous.

T F 25. The great lesson of social psychology is that persons and situations interact.

MULTIPLE-CHOICE PRACTICE TEST

Circle the correct letter.

1. Norms, according to the text,

    a. are composed of a set of roles
    b. prescribe proper behavior
    c. are social behaviors of typical or average people
    d. are laws that govern the distribution of social rewards

2. Which of the following is true?

    a. there are really no truly universal norms
    b. religion does not exist in some societies
    c. norms can restrain us so subtly that we hardly sense their existence
    d. a "pedestrian" would be an example of a role

3. "Personal space" refers to

    a. the property that a person owns, for example, a house and its grounds
    b. the favorite place a person retreats to when privacy is desired
    c. the exact spot that each person occupies, for example, the seats students occupy in a classroom
    d. the buffer zone that people like to maintain around their bodies

4. The cultural perspective highlights the importance of _____ in explaining the diversity of languages, customs, and expressive behaviors across the world.

   a. natural selection
   b. role playing
   c. hormonal factors
   d. human adaptability

5. Roger Brown's "universal norm" is

   a. the incest taboo
   b. that we relate to people of higher status the way we do to strangers, and to people of lower status the way we do to intimate friends
   c. that people the world over tend to relate to people of inferior status in the ways they relate to strangers
   d. the prohibition of theft

6. The enduring behaviors, ideas, attitudes, and traditions shared by a large group of people and transmitted from one generation to the next defines

   a. social roles
   b. coevolution
   c. ingroup bias
   d. a culture

7. Which of the following demonstrates that role-playing can be constructive?

   a. role reversal
   b. androgynous roles
   c. role diffusion
   d. communitarianism

8. The case of Patty Hearst illustrates

   a. the powerful effect of roles
   b. how natural selection predisposes psychological traits
   c. how role reversal promotes altruism
   d. the process of coevolution

9. Which of the following friendship norms seems to be universal?

   a. be prompt in keeping appointments with a friend
   b. respect the friend's privacy
   c. help the friend find a suitable spouse
   d. ask the friend's opinion before making a major decision

10. Cross-cultural studies of sexual behaviors indicate that

   a. with few exceptions males are more likely than females to initiate sexual relations
   b. in most societies males and females are equally likely to initiate sexual relations
   c. in societies where females outnumber males, females initiate sexual relations
   d. in third world countries females are more likely than males to initiate sexual relations

11. The study of how natural selection predisposes adaptive traits and behavior is called

    a. behavioral genetics   c. evolutionary psychology
    b. biological behaviorism   d. genetic psychology

12. Research indicates that a gender difference exists in

    a. vocabulary   c. age at which infants walk
    b. intelligence   d. smiling

13. According to Alice Eagly, biology and culture contribute to sex differences in behavior

    a. by influencing the roles people play
    b. by directly determining the personal traits of males and females
    c. through the process of natural selection
    d. by influencing the verbal and nonverbal communication styles of males and females

14. In essentially every known society,

    a. men are socially dominant
    b. men are more verbally fluent
    c. there are more male than female physicians
    d. males are responsible for finding enough food to eat

15. Critics have suggested that evolutionary psychology is characterized by

    a. the base-rate fallacy
    b. counterfactual thinking
    c. hindsight bias
    d. regression toward the average

16. _____ is more common in boys than in girls.

    a. Anxiety   c. Empathy
    b. Depression   d. Hyperactivity

17. A noticeable difference has <u>not</u> been found between males and females in

    a. happiness
    b. judging emotion on people's faces
    c. suicide rate
    d. frequency of smiling

18. According to evolutionary psychologists, which of the following is most fundamental to understanding the development of social behavior?

   a. cultural norms
   b. hormonal factors
   c. natural selection
   d. brain organization

19. Research on possible hormonal influences on aggression has indicated that

   a. testosterone levels influence animal aggression but not human aggression
   b. violent male criminals have higher than normal testosterone levels
   c. gender differences in aggression are clearly unrelated to hormonal differences
   d. administering testosterone reduces aggression in most animals

20. Who of the following maintain the least personal space?

   a. British
   b. Americans
   c. Arabs
   d. Scandinavians

21. Research on gender differences suggests that _____ are better at reading others' emotions and _____ are better at expressing emotions nonverbally.

   a. women; women
   b. women; men
   c. men; women
   d. men; men

22. A set of behavior expectations for males or females is a

   a. gender norm
   b. sex-role preference
   c. gender assignment
   d. gender role

23. Compared to college women who expected to meet a sexist male college senior, those women expecting to meet a male who presumably liked strong, ambitious women

   a. demonstrated a confused sense of gender identity
   b. performed more intelligently on a problem-solving task
   c. demonstrated stronger ethnic prejudice
   d. perceived other women as less empathic, competent, and friendly

24. According to the text, which of the following is true of the biological and cultural perspectives?

   a. biological and cultural factors are independent of one another
   b. biological and cultural perspectives are contradictory
   c. biological and cultural factors interact
   d. biological and cultural perspectives are actually identical

25. Research on conversational styles indicates that

    a. men's and women's conversational styles vary with the social context
    b. women are more fluent than men
    c. women are more likely to use the active than passive voice
    d. men and women are from different planets

26. A study of Australian married couples found that marital satisfaction was highest when

    a   both partners possessed feminine traits
    b. both partners possessed androgynous traits
    c. both partners possessed masculine traits
    d. the male possessed feminine traits and the female possessed masculine traits

27. A social role is defined by a whole cluster of _____ that accompany a social position.

    a. schemas   c. traits
    b. biases   d. norms

28. Research indicates that a gender difference does not exist in

    a. vocabulary   c. rate of violent crime
    b. sexual attitudes   d. social dominance

29. Research in developmental psychology indicates that

    a. genetic influences explain about 70 percent of our individual variations in personality traits
    b. siblings are as different from one another as are pairs of children selected randomly from the population
    c. the home is the most important influence in shaping a child's personality traits
    d. children and youth learn their games, musical tastes, and even their dirty words mostly from their siblings

30. Which of the following is true of the relationship between persons and situations?

    a. a given situation affects different people differently
    b. people choose many of their situations
    c. people help create the situations that affect them
    d. all of the above are true

31. As people mature to middle age and beyond,

    a. both men and women become more androgynous
    b. women but not men become more androgynous
    c. men but not women become more androgynous
    d. both men and women become less androgynous

32. In response to the question, "Do you think it is wrong for unmarried couples to bear children?" a 1997 World Gallup poll reported that

    a. the majority of people in all cultures surveyed said, "Yes"
    b. a minority of people in all cultures surveyed said, "Yes"
    c. about half the people in each culture surveyed said, "Yes"
    d. the percentage of people who said "yes" varied enormously from culture to culture

33. By lottery, people became either managers or clerks in a simulated business office. After the managers gave orders and performed higher-level work both the managers and clerks

    a. experienced a higher sense of self-efficacy
    b. experienced burnout
    c. viewed the managers as undeserving of their role
    d. viewed the managers as more intelligent, assertive, and supportive

34. Which of the following illustrates Roger Brown's "universal norm"?

    a. brothers do not have sexual relations with their sisters in Daneria
    b. the King of Sindab invites subjects to his castle for dinner before they invite him to their huts for dinner
    c. friends in Transylvania do not divulge things said in confidence
    d. males rather than females initiate sexual relations in Wallonia

35. William is gentle and affectionate with his children but independent and assertive in running his business. What term best describes his personality?

    a. androgynous   c. gender schematic
    b. gender diffused   d. interrole patterned

36. "Drivers are expected to keep to the right on a two-lane road" would be an example of what the text calls a

    a. norm   c. position
    b. role   d. status

37. Which of the following would be least likely to be considered a role?

a. college president
b. bicyclist
c. father
d. wife

38. The evolutionary perspective is to the cultural perspective as _____ is to _____

a. gender role; social role
b. coevolution; empathy
c. role; norm
d. human kinship; human diversity

39. Research suggests that 12-year-old Rafael is most likely to become a smoker if

a. his parents smoke
b. his friends smoke
c. his brothers smoke
d. his sisters smoke

40. In terms of the process of gender socialization, girls are to _____ as boys are to _____.

a. legs; arms
b. flowers; stems
c. bread; butter
d. roots; wings

SHORT ESSAY QUESTIONS

Answer the following questions in the space provided.

1. Contrast the evolutionary and cultural perspectives on human similarities and differences.

2. Define a "norm" and give one specific example of how norms vary by culture.

3. Describe Roger Brown's universal norm.

4. Define the concept of "role" and discuss the positive and negative effects of role-playing

5. Discuss three important gender differences.

6. Discuss the evolutionary psychologist's perspective on gender differences

7. Describe how gender roles vary with culture and over time.

8. What conclusion does the text reach regarding the relationship between biological and cultural influences?

9. Describe three ways in which persons and situations interact.

ANSWER KEY

Chapter Review

1. diversity
   similarities
   differences
   evolutionary
   cultural

2. natural
   genes
   universal

3. learn
   culture

4. rules
   grease
   personal
   less

5. universal
   status
   lower
   higher
   intimacy

6. norms
   superior
   subservient
   reversal

7. boys
   girls
   tasks
   relationships
   empathy
   emotions

8. dominant
   aggression
   sexual

9. aggression
   sexual
   fertility
   status
   testosterone
   shrink

10. expectations
    culture
    variations
    time
    peers

11. Biological
    cultural
    accentuate
    interact

12. interact
    react
    choose
    create

Matching Terms

1. k
2. g
3. b
4. d
5. m
6. f
7. a

8. e
9. l
10. i
11. h
12. c
13. j
14. n

True-False Review

1.	T	14.	T
2.	T	15.	T
3.	F	16.	T
4.	F	17.	F
5.	T	18.	T
6.	T	19.	F
7.	T	20.	T
8.	F	21.	T
9.	F	22.	F
10.	T	23.	T
11.	T	24.	T
12.	F	25.	T
13.	T		

Multiple-Choice Practice Test

1.	b	21.	a
2.	c	22.	d
3.	d	23.	b
4.	d	24.	c
5.	b	25.	a
6.	d	26.	a
7.	a	27.	d
8.	a	28.	a
9.	b	29.	b
10.	a	30.	d
11.	c	31.	a
12.	d	32.	d
13.	a	33.	d
14.	a	34.	b
15.	b	35.	a
16.	d	36.	a
17.	a	37.	b
18.	c	38.	d
19.	b	39.	b
20.	c	40.	d

CHAPTER 6

CONFORMITY

CHAPTER OBJECTIVES

After completing your study of this chapter you should be able to:

1. Define conformity and explain the difference between "compliance" and "acceptance."

2. Describe the findings of three classic studies on conformity.

3. Identify circumstances that are conducive to conformity.

4. Explain why people conform.

5. Indicate how personality and cultural background are related to conformity.

6. Explain why people sometimes resist social pressure.

CHAPTER REVIEW

Supply the words necessary to complete each of the following statements.

1. Conformity is change in _____ or _____ as a result of real or imagined group _____.

2. Conformity comes in two forms: _____ is publicly acting in accord with social pressure while privately disagreeing. _____ is both acting and believing in accord with social pressure.

CLASSIC STUDIES

3. Sherif found that estimates of the _____ phenomenon, the apparent movement of a stationary point of light in the dark, were easily influenced by the _____ of others. The group _____ lasted over long periods of time and succeeding generations of subjects.

4. Asch had individuals listen to others estimate which of three comparison _____ matched the standard. Although others gave an obviously _____ response, participants conformed 37 percent of the time.

5. Milgram investigated the degree to which people would obey an authority's instructions to deliver what were presumably traumatizing _____ _____ to another person in an adjacent room. Under optimum conditions—a _____, close-at-hand commander, a _____ victim, and no one else to exemplify disobedience—65 percent of adult male participants fully complied.

6. The conformity studies illustrate at least three social-psychological principles discussed in earlier chapters: The impact of behavior on _____, the power of the _____ to shape action, and the _____ attribution error.

WHEN DO PEOPLE CONFORM?

7. Conformity is influenced by several characteristics of the group. It is highest when the group is composed of _____ or more persons, is cohesive, is unanimous in its judgment, and is high in _____.

8. People also conform more when their responses are _____ and when they have not previously _____ themselves to a particular position.

WHY CONFORM?

9. People conform for two reasons: _____ influence is based on a person's desire to fulfill others' expectations, often to gain acceptance. _____ influence is conformity that results from accepting evidence about reality provided by other people.

WHO CONFORMS?

10. Researchers in the 1980s found that personality traits predict social behaviors such as conformity when measured across many _____. Personality also predicts behavior when social influences are _____. _____ differences in conformity suggest that people can be socialized to be more or less socially responsive.

RESISTING SOCIAL PRESSURE

11. Blatant attempts at social coercion produce _____—a motive to protect or restore one's sense of freedom. The reactance phenomenon reassures us that people are not _____.

12. People are uncomfortable when they appear too different from others, but neither do they want to appear the _____ as everyone else. Thus they will often act to preserve their sense of _____ and individuality.

MATCHING TERMS

Write the letter of the correct term from the right before the appropriate number on the left

_____ 1. A "we feeling"—the extent to which members of a group are bound together, such as by attraction for one another.

_____ 2. Conformity that results from accepting evidence about reality provided by other people.

_____ 3. A motive to protect or preserve one's sense of freedom.

_____ 4. Most people indicate their distinctive attributes.

_____ 5. The apparent movement of a stationary point of light in a dark room.

_____ 6. Studied obedience to authority.

_____ 7. A change in behavior or belief as a result of real or imagined group pressure.

_____ 8. Social contagion produced by a face-rubbing or foot-shaking person.

_____ 9. The underestimation of social forces.

_____ 10. An accomplice of the experimenter.

_____ 11. Used judgments of the lengths of lines to study conformity.

_____ 12. Conformity based on a person's desire to fulfill others' expectations, often to gain acceptance.

_____ 13. Used the autokinetic phenomenon to study conformity.

a. conformity

b. Sherif

c. autokinetic phenomenon

d. confederate

e. Asch

f. the chameleon effect

g. Milgram

h. cohesiveness

i. normative influence

j. informational influence

k. fundamental attribution error

l. reactance

m. spontaneous self-concept

TRUE-FALSE REVIEW

Circle T if the statement is true and F if it is false.

T F   1.   Conformity is sometimes good and sometimes bad.

T F   2.   Compliance and acceptance are different forms of conformity.

T F   3.   Fatal auto accidents and private airplane crashes increase after well-publicized suicides.

T F   4.   A confederate who made an inflated estimate of the autokinetic phenomenon had no effect on the judgments of naive participants.

T F   5.   In Asch's study involving the judgment of length of lines, the correct answer was obvious.

T F   6.   Asch's experimental procedure had "mundane" but not "experimental" realism.

T F   7.   "Mood linkage" refers to the genetic basis of emotion.

T F   8.   Milgram found that a total of 37 percent of male participants fully complied with the experimenter's commands.

T F   9.   When Milgram's experiment was repeated in a rundown office building in Bridgeport the percent of the participants who fully complied to the commands of the experimenter remained unchanged.

T F   10.   In the Milgram obedience studies, people of lower status tended to accept the experimenter's commands more readily than people of higher status.

T F   11.   When surveyed afterwards, most of Milgram's participants said they regretted having volunteered to participate in his study.

T F   12.   Compliance can breed acceptance.

T F   13.   The conformity research indicates that evil has its basis in some character defect.

T F   14.   In experiments on decision making by simulated juries, hung juries are more likely when jurors are polled by a show of hands rather than by secret ballot.

T F   15.   Two groups of three people elicit more conformity than one group of six.

T F   16.   Group members who feel attracted to the group are more responsive to the group's influence.

T F 17. After university women gave some thought to how traditional culture expects women to behave, they became more likely to exhibit traditional feminine modesty.

T F 18. People conform more when they must respond in the presence of others than when allowed to write down their answers privately.

T F 19. Normative social influence results from a person's desire to find meaning in life.

T F 20. Given a light touch on the arm, people are more likely to lend a dime or sample a new pizza.

T F 21. Replications of Asch's experiment in Britain, Canada, and the United States typically trigger more conformity than Asch observed two or three decades earlier.

T F 22. Knowing people's cultural backgrounds helps us predict how conforming they are.

T F 23. In Japan, going along with others is a sign of maturity.

T F 24. The theory of psychological reactance states that people desire consistency in their lives.

T F 25. When people are asked, "Tell us about yourself," they are most likely to report characteristics they share in common with others.

MULTIPLE-CHOICE PRACTICE TEST

Circle the correct letter.

1. _____ is a change in behavior or belief as a result of group pressure.

    a. Cohesiveness   c. Compliance
    b. Conformity   d. Obedience

2. Publicly acting in accord with social pressure while privately disagreeing is called

    a. acceptance   c. reactance
    b. compliance   d. interaction

3. Both acting and believing in accord with social pressure is called

    a. acceptance   c. compliance
    b. reactance   d. interaction

4. An important difference between Asch's experiment in which participants judged the length of lines and Sherif's experiment in which participants judged the movement of light was that

a Asch's participants were older than were Sherif's
b. there was an obviously correct answer in judging the length of lines, but that was not so in judging the movement of light
c. Asch's participants made their judgments privately whereas Sherif's participants made their judgments publicly
d. Asch's participants were all male whereas Sherif's participants were both male and female

5. In Asch's study of perceptual judgment involving the length of lines, naive participants conformed _____ of the time to the false judgments of the confederates.

a. 10 percent
b. 37 percent
c. 68 percent
d. 92 percent

6. In using the autokinetic phenomenon, Jacobs and Campbell found that when a confederate gave an inflated estimate of how far the light moved

a. naive participants were not influenced by the confederate's estimate
b. naive participants who heard the estimate were influenced but new members who joined were not
c. the confederate's judgment not only had an immediate influence but the inflated illusion persisted for five generations
d. the confederate's judgment had no immediate influence on group members but did have a delayed effect by shaping the estimates of group members after they left the group

7. Studies involving _____ most clearly demonstrate social influence taking the form of acceptance.

a. judgments of the length of lines
b. judgments of the autokinetic phenomenon
c. shocking innocent victims
d. administration of a drug overdose

8. Participants' tendencies to obey the experimenter's commands to shock a victim were highest when the experimenter was _____ and the victim was _____.

a. close; distant
b. close; close
c. distant; distant
d. distant; close

95

9. When the study of obedience was moved from Yale University to Bridgeport, Connecticut, the number of people who complied

    a. decreased from 65 percent to 48 percent
    b. decreased from 75 percent to 25 percent
    c. increased from 37 percent to 50 percent
    d. decreased from 37 percent to 10 percent

10. In a Pennsylvania State University experiment in which students were asked to predict how they would respond to a male's sexist comments, a _____ of students said they would ignore them. When other students actually heard such sexist remarks being made, a _____ of students said nothing.

    a. minority; minority   c. majority; minority
    b. minority; majority   d. majority; majority

11. A psychiatrist who interviewed 40 of Milgram's participants a year after their participation concluded that

    a. none had been harmed
    b. many were suspicious of all authorities
    c. a minority had lowered self-esteem
    d. most regretted having served in Milgram's study

12. When hospital nurses were called by an unknown physician and ordered to administer an obvious overdose of a drug,

    a. the majority of nurses did not comply and reported the incident to their supervisor
    b. the inexperienced nurses complied while the more experienced challenged the order
    c. most indicated to the physician that he would have to come in to sign the order before they could comply
    d. all but one proceeded to comply without delay

13. Which of the following social-psychological principles is <u>not</u> illustrated by the conformity literature?

    a. behavior shapes attitudes
    b. the fundamental attribution error
    c. the inoculation effect
    d. the power of the situation

14. To believe that Asch's compliant participants were particularly spineless people is to

    a. forget that behavior shapes belief
    b. overlook other personality characteristics that determine conformity
    c. make the fundamental attribution error
    d. ignore how the status of the experimenter shapes behavior

15. How social pressure may lead us to perform immoral acts is best illustrated by studies of

    a. psychological reactance   c. obedience to authority
    b. spontaneous self-concept   d. informational influence

16. Increasing the size of the group from _____ to _____ is likely to produce the greatest increase in conformity.

    a. 1000 to 2000   c. 2 to 5
    b. 50 to 100   d. 5 to 10

17. According to the text, suggestibility on a mass scale was evident in

    a. the wave of flying saucer sightings during the summer of 1949
    b. the "ethnic cleansings" occurring in Iraq and Bosnia
    c. the use of torture by the military junta in Greece during the early 1970s
    d. Le Chambon's sheltering of the Jews during the Holocaust

18. Conformity is highest when the response is _____ and _____.

    a. private; made without prior commitment
    b. public; made without prior commitment
    c. nonverbal; made in response to inanimate objects
    d. insignificant; made with prior commitment

19. Milgram reported that a participant's tendency to obey the experimenter decreased dramatically

    a. when two other participants defied the experimenter
    b. when the participant could not hear the responses of the learner
    c. when the experimenter was a female
    d. when the experimenter was younger than the participant

20. The training of torturers by the military junta in Greece in the early 1970s illustrates

    a. psychological reactance
    b. the inoculation effect
    c. the foot-in-the-door phenomenon
    d. the role of personality in conformity

21. Normative influence is to informational influence as _____ is to
    _____.

    a. autokinetic effect; cohesiveness
    b. compliance; acceptance
    c. conformity; reactance
    d. acceptance; reactance

22. _____ is based on a person's desire to be correct.

    a. Indirect influence
    b. Nominal influence
    c. Normative influence
    d. Informational influence

23. _____ is based on a person's desire to be accepted by the group.

    a. Indirect influence
    b. Nominal influence
    c. Normative influence
    d. Informational influence

24. Which of the following is true regarding individual differences in conformity?

    a. obedience rates in Austria and Italy are much lower than in the United States
    b. French participants conform less than Norwegian participants
    c. people's self-esteem test scores are excellent predictors of conformity
    d. American participants conform slightly more than German participants

25. Research indicates that personality is a better predictor of behavior when the people studied
    are _____ and when the social influences are _____.

    a. similar; strong
    b. similar; weak
    c. diverse; strong
    d. diverse; weak

26. Psychological reactance theory provides an explanation for

    a. resistance to authority
    b. obedience to authority
    c. why compliance is more common than acceptance
    d. why people are most likely to conform when the group is unanimous

27. In studying the impact of a confederate who occasionally rubbed her face or shook her foot,
    Tanya Chartrand and John Bargh found evidence of

    a. reactance
    b. normative social influence
    c. a chameleon effect
    d. the fundamental attribution error

28. Studies of people's spontaneous self-concepts indicate that

    a. they see themselves as better than average
    b. they react to blatant social pressure
    c. females define themselves in terms of their similarities while males define themselves in terms of their differences
    d. people value their uniqueness

29. Research has indicated that the number of suicides increases following

    a. well-publicized suicides
    b. a world war
    c. the Olympic games
    d. an economic recession

30. When Asch's conformity experiment has been repeated in other countries, the highest rate of conformity has been found in

    a. Lebanon
    b. the Bantu of Zimbabwe
    c. Hong Kong
    d. Brazil

31. Compared to Euro-American cultures, Asian cultures are more likely to teach their children

    a. independence
    b. collectivism
    c. to follow their own conscience
    d. to respect another's privacy

32. People who observed a lone individual in a group of four misjudge blue stimuli as green were subsequently

    a. more likely to conform to a group's erroneous judgments
    b. less likely to conform to a group's erroneous judgments
    c. less likely to value individualism
    d. more likely to value wisdom

33. After hearing a respected medical authority lecture about the value of eating fresh fruits and vegetables, Joshua includes more of them in his diet. This change in Joshua's eating patterns is an example of

    a. normative social influence
    b. psychological reactance
    c. informational social influence
    d. social facilitation

34. Peter hates to wear ties anywhere. Nevertheless he wears one to his sister's wedding to avoid the disapproval of his family. This is an example of

    a. identification
    b. informational social influence
    c. normative social influence
    d. psychological reactance

35. Ancient astronomers who observed the stars occasionally saw a star that seemed to move very abruptly. This is probably an example of

    a. the autokinetic effect
    b. the inoculation effect
    c. astronomical impact theory
    d. normative social influence

36. In light of the Milgram studies, to believe that soldiers who shoot innocent civilians as a consequence of following orders are unusually cruel is to

    a. make the fundamental attribution error
    b. engage in self-serving bias
    c. overlook the effect of cultural differences on conformity
    d. underestimate the influence of personality differences on conformity

37. Philip hates to attend concerts but goes because his wife wants to. After three years, Philip comes to genuinely enjoy concerts. This is an example of

    a. how acceptance can lead to compliance
    b. how compliance can lead to acceptance
    c. the "boomerang effect"
    d. how psychological reactance can lead to acceptance

38. Presidents rarely shift their positions on major foreign policy matters. This may be an example of how

    a. a "we-they" feeling has emerged between the major political parties
    b. public commitment reduces susceptibility to social influence
    c. high self-esteem is strongly related to nonconformity
    d. emotional distance from victims leads to disregard for their welfare

39. Milly generally likes to go home to visit her family during vacation. However, after her father tells her she must be home during spring vacation, Milly decides to remain at college We can probably best understand Milly's behavior in terms of

    a. reaction formation
    b. regression
    c. psychological reactance
    d. self-serving bias

40. John has red hair, has two brothers, one sister, and was born in Chicago. Both his parents were born in this country and are lawyers. If you asked John to "tell us about yourself," he is most likely to mention that

    a. he has two brothers
    b. he has red hair
    c. his father has a college education
    d. he was born in this country

SHORT ESSAY QUESTIONS

Answer the following questions in the space provided.

1. Define conformity. Explain the distinction between compliance and acceptance.

2. Briefly describe how each of the following investigators attempted to study conformity

   A. Sherif

   B. Asch

   C. Milgram

3. Identify three factors that are important to understanding <u>when</u> people conform.

4. Give two reasons <u>why</u> people conform.

5. Identify two personal characteristics that are important to understanding <u>who</u> conforms

6. Give two explanations for why people sometimes resist influence

Matching Terms

1. h	8. f
2. j	9. k
3. l	10. d
4. m	11. e
5. c	12. i
6. g	13. b
7. a	

True-False Review

1. T	14. T
2. T	15. T
3. T	16. T
4. F	17. F
5. T	18. T
6. F	19. F
7. F	20. T
8. F	21. F
9. F	22. T
10. T	23. T
11. F	24. F
12. T	25. F
13. F	

Multiple-Choice Practice Test

1. b	21. b
2. b	22. d
3. a	23. c
4. b	24. b
5. b	25. d
6. c	26. a
7. b	27. c
8. a	28. d
9. a	29. a
10. b	30. b
11. a	31. b
12. d	32. b
13. c	33. c
14. c	34. c
15. c	35. a
16. c	36. a
17. a	37. b
18. b	38. b
19. a	39. c
20. c	40. b

CHAPTER 7

PERSUASION

CHAPTER OBJECTIVES

After completing your study of this chapter you should be able to:

1. Identify the two paths to persuasion.

2. Describe communicator characteristics that contribute to effective communication.

3. Explain how the content of the message influences its effectiveness.

4. Describe the effects of different channels of communication.

5. Identify characteristics of the audience that influence susceptibility to persuasion.

6. Discuss the persuasion principles utilized in cult indoctrination.

7. Explain how people may resist persuasion.

CHAPTER REVIEW

Supply the words necessary to complete each of the following statements.

THE PATHS TO PERSUASION

1. Central route persuasion occurs when interested people focus on _____ and respond with favorable _____. Peripheral route persuasion occurs when people use rule-of-thumb _____ or incidental _____ to make snap judgments.

THE ELEMENTS OF PERSUASION

2. The four factors extensively studied in research on persuasion have been the
_____, the message, _____ the message is communicated, and
the _____.

3. Credible communicators are both _____ and _____. People
who speak _____ and look listeners straight in the eye are
viewed as more credible. Trustworthiness is also increased if the audience believes the
communicator is not trying to persuade them, argues against his or her own
_____, and _____ fast.

4. _____ communicators, for example, those with physical appeal or who
are similar to the audience, are also persuasive. Similar communicators are more
effective on matters of _____ than on judgments of_____.

5. Messages are more convincing when associated with _____
_____. Messages that arouse _____ can also be
effective especially when the listener is given effective ways to reduce it.

6. The effect of _____ depends on the communicator's
credibility. Highly credible people elicit the most opinion change when they argue a
relatively _____ position. Less credible people are more
successful advocating a _____ position. Those highly
_____ in an issue also tend to accept a narrow range of views.

7. A one-sided appeal is more effective than a two-sided appeal when the audience
_____ with the message, and is _____ of
opposing arguments.

8. In terms of arguments being presented first or last, the most common finding has been a
_____ effect. However, when _____ separates
the two messages and if a _____ must be made immediately after
hearing the second side, a _____ effect is more likely.

9. Attitudes developed from active _____ are stronger than those shaped
by appeals passively received. Although the mass media are typically not as potent as
_____ influence, the media are effective when the issue is minor or
_____. Many of the media's effects operate in a
"_____ flow" of communication—from media to
_____ leaders to the rank and file.

10. People with _____ self-esteem are the easiest to influence. The
_____ of the audience is also important. We seem to form our basic
attitudes when young and carry them through adulthood.

11. What the audience is _____ while listening to a message will determine its impact. _____ an audience of a disagreeable message reduces persuasion by stimulating _____. On the other hand, _____ people while they hear a disagreeable message can increase _____ by interfering with counterarguing.

CASE STUDIES IN PERSUASION: CULT INDOCTRINATION

12. Cults strengthen members' commitment by utilizing the principle that compliance breeds _____. By gradually increasing demands, the cult exploits the _____ phenomenon.

13. Successful cults have a _____ leader and present a vivid, _____ message that is directed to people who are at a _____ point in their lives. The cult typically _____ members in like-minded groups.

RESISTING PERSUASION: ATTITUDE INOCULATION

14. A prior public _____ to one's position, stimulated perhaps by a _____ attack on the position, breeds resistance to later persuasion. The attack on one's belief stimulates one to develop _____ that immunize against further attacks.

MATCHING TERMS

Write the letter of the correct term from the right before the appropriate number on the left

_____ 1. Information presented first has the most influence.

_____ 2. Breeds counterarguing.

_____ 3. Produced by weak attacks on people's beliefs.

_____ 4. The impact of a noncredible person may increase over time.

_____ 5. Influential on matters of personal value.

_____ 6. Especially effective when coupled with specific recommendations.

_____ 7. Isolation from family and friends produces this.

_____ 8. Information presented last has the most influence.

_____ 9. How the media influence the rank and file.

_____ 10. Face-to-face, in writing, on film.

_____ 11. Occurs when people are influenced by incidental cues.

_____ 12. Determines the effect of "discrepant" messages.

_____ 13. Marshals systematic arguments to stimulate favorable thinking.

_____ 14. Process by which a message induces change in beliefs, attitudes, or behaviors.

a. sleeper effect

b. fear appeals

c. primacy effect

d. recency effect

e. communication channels

f. central route persuasion

g. attitude inoculation

h. communicator's credibility

i. persuasion

j. peripheral route persuasion

k. forewarning

l. two-step flow

m. similar communicators

n. social implosion

TRUE-FALSE REVIEW

Circle T if the statement is true and F if it is false.

T F 1. Several educational campaigns in different sections of the country have been successful in convincing motorists to use seat belts.

T F 2. Collegians' support for marijuana's legalization continues to dwindle.

T F 3. The term "sleeper effect" refers to the fact that what people are doing when a message is presented influences its effectiveness.

T F 4. Speakers who talk rapidly are generally seen as lacking in credibility.

T F 5. The central route to persuasion is best illustrated by advertisements that feature Hollywood stars.

T F 6. Dissimilar communicators are more effective than similar communicators on matters of objective reality.

T F 7. Communicators are viewed as more trustworthy if the audience believes they are not trying to persuade them.

T F 8. Researchers found that college students were more convinced by persuasive messages if allowed to enjoy peanuts and Pepsi while reading them.

T F 9. People rated trivial statements like "Mercury has a higher boiling point than copper" as more truthful if they had read and rated them a week before.

T F 10. Well-educated audiences are more responsive to rational appeals than are less-educated audiences.

T F 11. In comparison to the peripheral route, the central route to persuasion is more likely to lead to lasting attitude and behavioral change.

T F 12. When people's attitudes were formed primarily through emotion, they are more persuaded by intellectual rather than emotional appeals.

T F 13. A highly credible source elicits most opinion change by advocating a position moderately discrepant from the position held by the recipient.

T F 14. Two-sided arguments are more effective than one-sided arguments if the listener initially disagrees with the communicator's position.

T F 15. In terms of the order of arguments, a recency effect is more commonly found than a primacy effect.

T F 16. Television advertisements for aspirin are generally ineffective.

T F 17. Cult influence techniques are in some ways similar to techniques used by more familiar groups.

T F 18. Messages are best comprehended and recalled when written.

T F 19. The "two-step flow of communication" model has been used to explain the mass media's effect on the audience.

T F 20. Forewarning people that they will be exposed to a discrepant message reduces their susceptibility to it.

T F 21. The life-cycle explanation offers the best account of the generation gap.

T F 22. Cult leaders use the foot-in-the-door technique to gain behavior commitments.

T F 23. The group isolation that occurs in cults leads to "social implosion."

T F 24. "Attitude inoculation" is accomplished by offering people new arguments to bolster their existing attitudes.

T F 25. Being an active listener may build up one's resistance to persuasion.

MULTIPLE-CHOICE PRACTICE TEST

Circle the correct letter.

1. According to the text, persuasive attempts have probably been least effective in changing attitudes toward

   a. cigarette smoking
   b. marijuana use

   c. use of seat belts
   d. alcohol consumption

2. The central route is to _____ as the peripheral route is to _____.

   a. analytical; motivated
   b. similarity; attractiveness
   c. heuristics; incidental cues
   d. high effort; low effort

3. Social psychologists study persuasion primarily through

    a. experiments   c. case studies
    b. surveys   d. participant observation

4. Credible communicators are both _____ and _____.

    a. expert; attractive
    b. intelligent; mature
    c. attractive; intelligent
    d. expert; trustworthy

5. Communicators who talk fast and look the listener in the eye are likely to be perceived as more

    a. selfish   c. attractive
    b. manipulative   d. credible

6. Which of the following is one of the four major factors studied by psychologists in research on effective persuasion?

    a. the function of communication
    b. the setting of communication
    c. the channel of communication
    d. the length of communication

7. Which of the following most clearly demonstrates the "sleeper effect"?

    a. unsuspecting people often fail to distinguish education from propaganda
    b. a foreign language can be acquired by listening to records while one sleeps
    c. the impact of a noncredible person may increase over time
    d. people who are not alert rarely counterargue

8. Wood and Eagly reported that when a speaker presents _____ we are more likely to attribute the message to compelling evidence and thus to be persuaded by it.

    a. a popular rather than an unpopular position
    b. an unexpected rather than an expected position
    c. an emotional rather than a rational appeal
    d. a political rather than a religious position

9. People who argue against their own self-interest

    a. are effective in persuading a female audience but not in persuading a male audience
    b. are effective with an intelligent audience but not with an unintelligent audience
    c. are viewed as inconsistent and thus lose their effectiveness
    d. are viewed as more credible and are thus more influential

10. "Similar" communicators are more effective in persuading on _____ than on _____.

    a. radio; television
    b. judgments of fact; matters of value
    c. political issues; religious beliefs
    d. matters of value; judgments of fact

11. Research indicates that stimulating thinking in the audience makes strong messages _____ persuasive and weak messages _____ persuasive.

    a. more; more
    b. more; less
    c. less; more
    d. less; less

12. Dawn Wilson and her colleagues found that doctors' letters to patients who smoked were most influential if they explained that by

    a. continuing to smoke they would likely die sooner
    b. quitting they would live longer
    c. quitting their food would taste better
    d. quitting they would save money

13. A fear-arousing communication has been most effective in leading

    a. women to use sunscreen
    b. women to get mammograms
    c. men to eat healthy foods
    d. men to use condoms

14. Which factor has been shown to influence the impact a discrepant message has on the audience?

    a. age of the audience
    b. communication channel
    c. communicator credibility
    d. communicator attractiveness

15. American World War II soldiers initially opposed to a message suggesting that the Japanese would not be easily defeated were more persuaded by a _____ communication. Soldiers initially agreeing with the message were strengthened more by a _____ message.

    a. videotaped; written
    b. one-sided; two-sided
    c. emotional; rational
    d. two-sided; one-sided

16. When two persuasive messages are presented back-to-back and the audience responds at some later time,

    a. a primacy effect occurs
    b. a recency effect occurs
    c. a primacy effect occurs with rational appeals, but a recency effect occurs with emotional appeals
    d. social implosion occurs

17. Persuasion studies have shown that the major influence upon our most important beliefs and attitudes is

    a. television and radio
    b. the school
    c. the church
    d. our contact with people

18. Highly credible communicators elicit most opinion change when they advocate positions that

    a. differ only moderately from the position of the audience
    b. differ extensively from the position of the audience
    c. elicit strong reactance from the audience
    d. arouse strong dissonance in the audience

19. The mass media's persuasive power is most noticeable on

    a. religious beliefs
    b. matters of objective fact
    c. political values
    d. minor or unfamiliar issues

20. The results of one study indicated that easy-to-understand messages were most persuasive when _____ while difficult messages were most persuasive when _____.

    a. audiotaped; written
    b. written; presented live
    c. videotaped; written
    d. videotaped; audiotaped

21. When researchers went to the homes of people from 12 churches shortly after they heard sermons opposing racial bigotry, they found that _____ percent spontaneously recalled the sermons.

   a. 10
   b. 30
   c. 50
   d. 70

22. What effect does distraction have on persuasive communications?

   a. distraction interferes with reception of the message and as a result the communication is always less persuasive
   b. distraction facilitates persuasion by inhibiting counterarguing
   c. the results of studies are so conflicting that no one knows
   d. distraction facilitates persuasion by reducing the sleeper effect

23. People may be more likely to be influenced by peripheral cues such as the appeal of the communicator when they are

   a. image-conscious and thus care less about whether they are right or wrong
   b. highly involved in the issue
   c. analytically inclined
   d. in genuine conflict over the merits of the arguments

24. "Life-cycle" and "generational" explanations both attempt to explain

   a. why the content of messages changes over time
   b. why people have different attitudes depending on their age
   c. why a particular communicator has a different effect on people of different ages
   d. how an emotional appeal builds to a climax in terms of its impact

25. According to the cult researcher Margaret Singer, youths from which class may be most trusting and thus vulnerable to a "credible" communicator?

   a. lower class
   b. middle class
   c. upper class
   d. all are equally vulnerable

26. According to the text, which age group is most vulnerable to cult indoctrination?

   a. under age 25
   b. between 25 and 35
   c. between 35 and 45
   d. over 60

27. Social implosion occurs in groups when

    a. ties with people outside the group weaken and each member interacts only with other group members
    b. a cult member overthrows the leader
    c. the poorer members assume leadership and the wealthy become the followers
    d. the cult seeks to attempt major changes in society

28. Attitude inoculation seeks to strengthen beliefs

    a. by giving supporting arguments for the beliefs
    b. by using different channels to communicate the same message
    c. by providing social support for the beliefs
    d. through a weak attack on the beliefs

29. According to the text, the inoculation research suggests that one can build up resistance to persuasion by

    a. listening only to rational appeals
    b. seeking social support for one's beliefs
    c. being an active listener
    d. ignoring emotional appeals

30. College students who live on campus report that they learn most from their contact with

    a. books
    b. professors
    c. newspapers and magazines
    d. friends and fellow students

31. Which of the following illustrates media influence through a two-step flow of communication?

    a. a teenager buys a shampoo he saw advertised both on television and in a favorite magazine
    b. a gun manufacturer convinces a television station to broadcast a program on the right of citizens to bear arms
    c. a candidate for political office answers questions from a live audience on television
    d. a salesman purchases a new car after talking to a respected friend who read about its advantages in a consumers' magazine

32. Forewarning people that they are going to be exposed to a persuasive communication

    a. distracts them and thus makes them more susceptible to influence
    b. generally has no effect on their susceptibility to influence
    c. elicits fear and reduces their comprehension of the message
    d. makes them more resistant to influence

33. People who are highly involved in an issue will likely be most influenced by the

    a. attractiveness of the source
    b. expertise of the source
    c. strength of the arguments
    d. sheer number of arguments

34. An attractive or similar communicator would be most effective in changing beliefs about the

    a. health benefits of eating fruits and vegetables
    b. dangers of marijuana use
    c. dangers of driving without wearing seatbelts
    d. advantages of living in a small town versus the country or a large city

35. According to the text, inoculation procedures have been successfully used in helping

    a. motorists to use seat belts
    b. citizens to work for nuclear disarmament
    c. young people to resist peer pressure to smoke
    d. the elderly to resist political pressures to reduce Social Security benefits

36. A gun manufacturer delivers a speech against stricter gun legislation. Because he clearly has a vested interest, his arguments have little initial impact on the audience. However, several weeks later, a survey of the audience indicates that his impact was much greater than first thought. This would be an example of

    a. the recency effect   c. social implosion
    b. the sleeper effect   d. attitude inoculation

37. You have been asked to design an advertising campaign urging people to stop smoking. To be most effective your message should arouse

    a. no fear   c. a low level of fear
    b. a moderate level of fear   d. a high level of fear

38. You have been asked to prepare a speech opposing capital punishment. To be most effective in convincing those who strongly favor the death penalty you should present

    a. a one-sided communication   c. an emotional appeal
    b. a two-sided communication   d. an audiotaped appeal

116

39. You are one of two candidates being interviewed for a position as superintendent of the city school system. You are notified that one candidate will be interviewed tomorrow evening and the other a week later. The school board will make a decision immediately after the second candidate has been interviewed. If you want the job

    a. you should try to be interviewed first
    b. you should try to be interviewed last
    c. you should try to be interviewed first but only if the school board is composed of college graduates and the other candidate is controversial
    d. you should try to be interviewed first but only if you are more attractive than the other candidate

40. According to research presented in the text, the mass media may be most effective in shaping

    a. whether one becomes a Democrat or Republican
    b. whether a person believes in God or not
    c. the brand of shampoo a person buys
    d. one's attitude toward capital punishment

SHORT ESSAY QUESTIONS

Answer the following questions in the space provided.

1. Briefly describe the two paths to persuasion.

2. List the four major factors psychologists have investigated in research on persuasion.

117

3. What factors may influence the perceived credibility of a communicator?

4. Briefly state the research findings regarding each of the following:

   A. Fear appeals

   B. Message discrepancy

   C. One-sided versus two-sided messages

   D. Primacy versus recency effects

5. Contrast the effectiveness of face-to-face personal influence and that of the mass media.

6. Describe how the principles of effective persuasion are implemented in cult indoctrination

7. Describe what is meant by attitude inoculation.

Chapter Review

1. arguments
   thoughts
   heuristics
   cues

2. communicator
   how
   audience

3. expert
   trustworthy
   confidently
   self-interest
   talks

4. Attractive
   value
   fact

5. good feelings
   fear

6. discrepancy
   extreme
   moderate
   involved

7. agrees
   unaware

8. primacy
   time
   commitment
   recency

9. experience
   personal
   unfamiliar
   two-step
   opinion

10. moderate
    age

11. thinking
    Forewarning
    counterarguing
    distracting
    persuasion

12. acceptance
    foot-in-the-door

13. charismatic
    emotional
    turning
    isolates

14. commitment
    mild
    counterarguments

Matching Terms

1. c
2. k
3. g
4. a
5. m
6. b
7. n

8. d
9. l
10. e
11. j
12. h
13. f
14. i

True-False Review

1.	F	14.	T
2.	F	15.	F
3.	F	16.	F
4.	F	17.	T
5.	F	18.	T
6.	T	19.	T
7.	T	20.	T
8.	T	21.	F
9.	T	22.	T
10.	T	23.	T
11.	T	24.	F
12.	F	25.	T
13.	F		

Multiple-Choice Practice Test

1.	c	21.	a
2.	d	22.	b
3.	a	23.	a
4.	d	24.	b
5.	d	25.	b
6.	c	26.	a
7.	c	27.	a
8.	b	28.	d
9.	d	29.	c
10.	d	30.	d
11.	d	31.	d
12.	a	32.	d
13.	b	33.	c
14.	c	34.	d
15.	d	35.	c
16.	a	36.	b
17.	d	37.	d
18.	b	38.	b
19.	d	39.	b
20.	c	40.	c

CHAPTER 8

GROUP INFLUENCE

CHAPTER OBJECTIVES

After completing your study of this chapter you should be able to:

1. Define a group.

2. Discuss how we are affected by the presence of others.

3. Identify the conditions under which social loafing is likely to occur.

4. Describe the psychological state of "deindividuation."

5. Define and explain group polarization.

6. Discuss the causes, symptoms, and prevention of "groupthink."

7. Identify the factors that strengthen minority influence and describe effective leadership

CHAPTER REVIEW

Supply the words necessary to complete each of the following statements.

WHAT IS A GROUP?

1. A group consists of _____ or more people who, for longer than a few moments, _____ with and influence one another and perceive one another as "us."

SOCIAL FACILITATION

2. The most elementary issue in social psychology concerns how we are affected by the mere _____ of other people. Some early experiments found that one's performance on simple arithmetic and verbal tasks _____

when either observers or co-actors were present. Other experiments found that others' presence can _____ one's performance.

3. Robert Zajonc reconciled the contradictory findings with a well-known principle from experimental psychology: Arousal facilitates _____ responses. Subsequent research indicated that the presence of others boosts performance on _____ tasks and hinders performance on _____ tasks.

4. Being in a crowd intensifies people's normally _____ or _____ reactions. In dense situations we may be more responsive to people's reactions. Crowding also enhances _____.

5. Experiments suggest that we are aroused by others partly as a result of _____ apprehension and partly from a _____ between paying attention to others and paying attention to the task. Other studies indicate that the presence of others can be _____ even when the actor is not being evaluated or distracted.

SOCIAL LOAFING

6. Social loafing may occur in work situations where people pool their efforts toward a _____ goal and where individuals are not _____ for their efforts. Laboratory experiments show that group members work less hard when performing "_____ tasks." When responsibility is diffused, individuals may attempt to _____-ride on the group effort.

7. Research indicates that group members loaf less when they are given _____ objectives, when they are _____ for group success, and when there is a spirit of _____ to the team.

DEINDIVIDUATION

8. When high levels of social arousal are combined with diffused _____, people may abandon their normal restraints and lose their sense of _____. Such "deindividuation" is likely when people can assume _____ by being in a large group or by wearing uniforms.

9. The loss of self-awareness is accompanied by increased responsiveness to the immediate _____, be it positive or negative. Similarly, circumstances that increase _____ will decrease deindividuation.

GROUP POLARIZATION

10. James Stoner discovered that group discussion tended to _____ risktaking. In seeking to explain the "risky shift," investigators discovered that discussion tends to _____ whatever is the initially dominant point of view.

11. Informational and normative influence explain why groups intensify _____. Group discussion elicits a pooling of persuasive _____ which favor the dominant point of view. In addition, social _____ with others reveals surprising support for one's initial inclination. To be perceived favorably, a person expresses stronger opinions.

GROUPTHINK

12. A group's desire for _____ can override its realistic appraisal of alternative courses of action. Irving Janis suggested that groupthink is most likely to occur when the group is cohesive, is _____ from contrary viewpoints, and has a_____ leader.

13. The symptoms of groupthink include (1) an _____ of invulnerability, (2) rationalization, (3) unquestioned belief in the group's _____, (4) _____ views of the opposition, (5) pressure to conform, (6) _____ of misgivings, (7) an illusion of unanimity, and (8) "_____" who protect the group from unpleasant information.

MINORITY INFLUENCE

14. Research indicates that a minority is most influential when it is _____ and persistent in its views, when its actions convey an image of _____, and when it elicits some defections from the majority. Even if it fails to persuade the majority to adopt its position, the minority may increase the majority's _____ and willingness to consider other alternatives. One example of the power of individuals is _____, the process by which certain group members motivate and guide the group. Research indicates that effective supervisors score high on tests of both _____ and _____ leadership.

MATCHING TERMS

Write the letter of the correct term from the right before the appropriate number on the left

_____ 1. Occurs on additive tasks.

_____ 2. Enhances a minority's influence.

_____ 3. People who benefit from the group but give little in return.

_____ 4. Discovered the risky shift.

_____ 5. A way of evaluating one's opinions and abilities.

_____ 6. The best supported explanation for group polarization.

_____ 7. Studied minority influence.

_____ 8. Was revised in favor of group polarization.

_____ 9. Occurs in groups that foster anonymity.

_____ 10. Studied groupthink.

_____ 11. The strengthening of dominant responses due to the presence of others.

_____ 12. Partially explains why the presence of others arouses us.

_____ 13. A false impression of how others are thinking or feeling.

_____ 14. A symptom of groupthink.

a. social comparison

b. deindividuation

c. free riders

d. social facilitation

e. social loafing

f. evaluation apprehension

g. risky shift

h. self-censorship

i. self-confidence

j. informational influence

k. Janis

l. pluralistic ignorance

m. Stoner

n. Moscovici

TRUE-FALSE REVIEW

Circle T if the statement is true and F if it is false.

T F 1. Social psychologists define a group as any collection of two or more individuals.

T F 2. "Co-actors" are people engaged in some competitive activity.

T F 3. The presence of others facilitates the performance of easy tasks and hinders performance of difficult tasks.

T F 4. The social-facilitation effect has been explained in terms of informational influence.

T F 5. College basketball players become slightly less accurate in their free-throw shooting in a packed fieldhouse.

T F 6. Researchers agree that all great leaders share common traits.

T F 7. Whenever people are in a crowd, they experience discomfort and stress.

T F 8. Some research indicates that effective supervisors score high on tests of both task and social leadership.

T F 9. Social loafing is not likely to occur in athletic contests where one individual competes against another.

T F 10. Social loafing seems to occur because of poor coordination of individual efforts within a group.

T F 11. The workers on Israel's communal kibbutz farms demonstrate social loafing.

T F 12. Social loafing decreases when the size of a group increases.

T F 13. Anonymity inevitably has a negative impact on group members.

T F 14. Research indicates that group discussion invariably increases risk taking.

T F 15. Studies of social loafing grew out of earlier research on the risky shift.

T F 16. "Group polarization" refers to a split within a group.

T F 17. Recent research suggests that cohesiveness is a more significant determinant of groupthink than is directive leadership.

T F 18. The concept of groupthink grew out of an analysis of poor decisions made in business and industry.

T F 19. A supportive audience always elicits better performance on skilled tasks.

T F 20. Groups of eyewitnesses give accounts of a crime that are much more accurate than those provided by isolated individuals.

T F 21. Brainstorming face-to-face generates more creative ideas than do the same people working alone.

T F 22. One prescription for preventing groupthink is to have one or more members assigned the role of devil's advocate.

T F 23. Laboratory research suggests that putting on a black jersey can lead wearers to behave more aggressively.

T F 24. According to the text, the <u>Challenger</u> disaster may have had its basis in a group decision characterized by groupthink.

T F 25. Researchers have found that a minority person who defected from the majority was even more persuasive than one who consistently voiced the minority position.

MULTIPLE-CHOICE PRACTICE TEST

Circle the correct letter.

1. Which form of social influence discussed in Chapter 9 does not necessarily involve an interacting group?

   a. group polarization
   b. groupthink
   c. minority influence
   d. social facilitation

2. The definition of a group given in the text and provided by Marvin Shaw states that a group consists of

   a. any collection of individuals
   b. two or more people who interact and influence one another
   c. two or more people who share similar values
   d. a collection of individuals that is cohesive

3. Which of the following is true?

   a. people's color preferences are stronger when they make judgments with others present
   b. ants excavate less sand in the presence of other ants
   c. in the presence of others, students take more time to learn a simple maze and less time to learn one that is complex
   d. joggers run more slowly when jogging with someone else

4. Early experiments found that the presence of others improved people's efficiency at

   a. learning nonsense syllables
   b. crossing out designated letters
   c. performing complex multiplication problems
   d. learning foreign language words

5. James Michaels and his colleagues found that in the presence of observers,

   a. good pool players shot better and poor pool players shot worse
   b. students playing checkers and chess played worse
   c. good pool players shot worse and poor pool players shot better
   d. students playing checkers played better and students playing chess played worse

6. Studies of the effect of other people on athletic performance have shown that

   a. college basketball players become slightly more accurate when highly aroused by a packed fieldhouse
   b. the drives of professional golfers are shorter when an audience is present
   c. home teams in baseball's World Series have won 60 percent of the final games
   d. in college and professional sports, home teams win about 6 in 10 games

7. In a study of university students in India, researchers found that crowding hampered performance only on _____ tasks.

   a. verbal   c. simple
   b. motor   d. complex

8. Research indicates that people perform best when their co-actor is

   a. not watching them   c. of the opposite sex
   b. slightly superior   d. highly competitive

9. Social facilitation and social loafing have been explained in terms of difference in

   a. evaluation concern   c. cognitive dissonance
   b. informational influence d. group polarization

10. Which process helps explain both social loafing and deindividuation?

    a. self-censorship
    b. minority influence
    c. diffusion of responsibility
    d. group polarization

11. Research indicates that being in a crowd _____ positive reactions and _____ negative reactions.

    a. intensifies; intensifies
    b. weakens; intensifies
    c. intensifies; weakens
    d. weakens; weakens

12. Which of the following is false?

    a. groups of friends loaf less than groups of strangers
    b. Israel's communal kibbutz farms have outproduced Israel's noncollective farms
    c. research completed in Japan, Thailand, and India indicates that social loafing does not occur in less individualistic, more group-centered cultures
    d. students pumped exercise bikes more energetically when they knew they were being individually monitored than when they thought their output was being pooled with that of other riders

13. Experiments show that people in groups loaf less when

    a. the task is challenging
    b. they are in an unfamiliar setting
    c. they have a strong sense of external control
    d. the task is routine

14. Women dressed in Ku Klux Klan-style coats and hoods were more aggressive than those who were visible and wearing name tags. This finding is best explained in terms of the process of

    a. groupthink
    b. deindividuation
    c. reactance
    d. social facilitation

15. The research on deindividuation shows that a group experience that diminishes people's self consciousness also tends to

    a. decrease their emotional arousal
    b. decrease their normal inhibitions
    c. increase their feelings of self-esteem
    d. increase their sensitivity to their own conscience

16. The term "risky shift" was used to refer to the finding of

    a. groups being riskier than individuals
    b. individuals being riskier than groups
    c. males being riskier than females
    d. people becoming less risky as they grow older

17. Studies of the risky shift eventually led to formulation of

    a. social comparison theory
    b. the group polarization hypothesis
    c. the social facilitation effect
    d. the social-loafing effect

18. Group polarization is most likely to occur in a group

    a. of like-minded people
    b. of unintelligent people
    c. of persons with differing value systems
    d. discussing political issues

19. Myers and Bishop set up groups of relatively prejudiced and unprejudiced high school students and asked them to respond both before and after discussion to issues involving racial attitudes. Results indicated that after discussion

    a. both groups were more prejudiced
    b. both groups were less prejudiced
    c. the individuals who were relatively unprejudiced became even less prejudiced and the individuals who were relatively prejudiced became even more prejudiced
    d. the individuals who were relatively unprejudiced became more prejudiced and the individuals who were relatively prejudiced became less prejudiced

20. According to the text, which of the following provides the best supported explanation for group polarization?

    a. social comparison theory
    b. informational influence
    c. diffusion of responsibility
    d. cognitive dissonance theory

21. According to Janis, which of the following was the product of groupthink?

    a. the Truman administration's formulation of the Marshall Plan after World War II
    b. the Truman administration's decision to drop the atomic bomb on Hiroshima
    c. the Johnson administration's decision to escalate the Vietnam War
    d. the Nixon administration's decision to freeze prices

22. An analysis of terrorist organizations around the world suggests that the extremist activities of these groups may be understood in terms of the process of

    a. social loafing   c. minority influence
    b. social facilitation   d. group polarization

23. Frank and Gilovich's laboratory research suggested that putting on a black uniform can produce

    a. social loafing   c. aggression
    b. groupthink   d. evaluation apprehension

24. Patrick Laughlin reported that if only two members of a six-person group are initially correct in solving an analogy problem, they

    a. rarely convince the others
    b. convince the others one-third of the time
    c. convince the others two-thirds of the time
    d. always convince the others

25. A directive leader is a contributing cause of

    a. deindividuation   c. groupthink
    b. responsibility diffusion d. the risky shift

26. Research suggests that minorities are less persuasive regarding _____ than regarding _____.

    a. fact; attitude   c. principle; practice
    b. attitude; fact   d. practice; principle

27. Which of the following is not a symptom of groupthink?

    a. unquestioned belief in the group's morality
    b. rationalization
    c. conformity pressure
    d. social loafing

28. Moscovici and his associates found that if a minority judges blue slides to be green,

    a. it has no effect on the judgments of the majority
    b. members of the majority will occasionally agree but only if the minority is consistent
    c. members of the majority demonstrate reactance by judging green slides to be blue
    d. female but not male members of the majority will occasionally agree

29. Groupthink occurs when group members desire

    a. control   c. power
    b. harmony   d. freedom

30. Research indicates that a minority member who _____ is persuasive.

    a. wavers
    b. has defected from the majority
    c. tends to be introverted
    d. appears impatient

31. Studies done in India, Taiwan, and Iran found that the most effective supervisors in coal mines, banks, and government offices scored

    a. high on both task and social leadership
    b. high on task and low on social leadership
    c. high on either task or social leadership but not high on both
    d. low on task and high on social leadership

32. Tom, a successful foreman in a large furniture factory, emphasizes the attainment of production goals and sets high standards for the workers under him. Tom's style is an example of _____ leadership.

    a. normative   c. autocratic
    b. task   d. Type A

33. The presence of others would be most likely to improve performance on

    a. raking up leaves
    b. solving crossword puzzles
    c. learning foreign language words
    d. solving complex mathematical puzzles

34. Who of the following would be considered co-actors?

    a. four people doing push-ups in an exercise class
    b. two people playing bridge
    c. eight competitors running a 5-kilometer race
    d. two children playing badminton

35. After an exciting soccer game in which the home team loses, a crowd of fans throws garbage and begins to tear up the field. This behavior is best understood in terms of

    a. group polarization   c. groupthink
    b. deindividuation   d. social facilitation

36. Which of the following is least likely to be considered a group as defined in the text?

    a. a husband and wife talking over dinner
    b. a committee of eight discussing the problem of neighborhood crime
    c. four seven-year-olds playing hide-and-go-seek
    d. seven people waiting at a bus stop

37. The presence of others would be least likely to improve performance in

    a. playing chess   c. running
    b. weightlifting   d. the broad jump

38. Social loafing would be least likely to occur

    a. in a boys' club trying to raise money by holding a Saturday car wash
    b. in a relay race where each team member's performance is timed
    c. in a community garden where each family is expected to contribute whatever free time they have
    d. in a work crew building a new highway

39. Individuals who tend to favor stiff penalties for drunk drivers come together to discuss various ways of dealing with the problem of intoxicated drivers. The group polarization hypothesis predicts that after group discussion,

    a. the individuals will favor even more severe penalties for drunk drivers
    b. the individuals will tend to become more tolerant of drunk drivers
    c. the individuals will be divided into two opposing groups as to the best way to deal with drunk drivers
    d. the individuals will favor a rehabilitation program rather than a jail sentence for drunk drivers

40. Which of the following is a comment you are least likely to hear made within a group characterized by groupthink?

    a. "Our critics are not very smart."
    b. "Our past decisions have always been right."
    c. "Let's make the decision and get out of here. I've got more important things to do."
    d. "It seems to me we are all in agreement on this, so let's proceed."

SHORT ESSAY QUESTIONS

Answer the following questions in the space provided.

1. Define a group.

2. Describe how the meaning of the term "social facilitation" has changed.

3. Explain what is meant by the term "free riders." When is free riding most likely to occur?

4. What is deindividuation? Briefly describe its causes and effects.

5. Provide two explanations for group polarization.

6. List the major symptoms of groupthink.

7. Identify two factors that contribute to the effectiveness of minority influence

ANSWER KEY

Chapter Review

1. two
   interact

2. presence
   improved
   hinder

3. dominant
   easy
   difficult

4. positive
   negative
   arousal

5. evaluation
   conflict
   arousing

6. common
   accountable
   additive
   free

7. challenging
   rewarded
   commitment

8. responsibility
   individuality
   anonymity

9. situation
   self-awareness

10. increase
    enhance

11. opinions
    arguments
    comparison

12. harmony
    isolated
    directive

13. illusion
    morality
    stereotyped
    self-censorship
    mindguards

14. consistent
    self-confidence
    self-doubts
    leadership
    task
    social

Matching Terms

1. e
2. i
3. c
4. m
5. a
6. j
7. n
8. g
9. b
10. k
11. d
12. f
13. l
14. h

True-False Review

1.	F	14.	F
2.	F	15.	F
3.	T	16.	F
4.	F	17.	F
5.	T	18.	F
6.	F	19.	F
7.	F	20.	T
8.	T	21.	F
9.	T	22.	T
10.	F	23.	T
11.	F	24.	T
12.	F	25.	T
13.	F		

Multiple-Choice Practice Test

1.	d	21.	c
2.	b	22.	d
3.	a	23.	c
4.	b	24.	c
5.	a	25.	c
6.	d	26.	a
7.	d	27.	d
8.	b	28.	b
9.	a	29.	b
10.	c	30.	b
11.	a	31.	a
12.	c	32.	b
13.	a	33.	a
14.	b	34.	a
15.	b	35.	b
16.	a	36.	d
17.	b	37.	a
18.	a	38.	b
19.	c	39.	a
20.	b	40.	c

CHAPTER 9

PREJUDICE: DISLIKING OTHERS

CHAPTER OBJECTIVES

After completing your study of this chapter you should be able to:

1. Distinguish between prejudice and discrimination.

2. Trace recent trends in racial and gender prejudice in the United States.

3. Explain how unequal status, self-fulfilling prophecy, and the mere formation of groups foster prejudice.

4. Demonstrate how prejudice is maintained through conformity and institutional supports.

5. Explain the scapegoat theory of prejudice and the personality dynamics of authoritarianism.

6. Show how stereotypes can be a by-product of our normal thinking processes.

7. Describe the just world phenomenon.

8. Identify cognitive consequences of stereotypes.

CHAPTER REVIEW

Supply the words necessary to complete each of the following statements.

THE NATURE AND POWER OF PREJUDICE

1. Prejudice is a negative _____ of a group and its individual members. The beliefs supporting prejudice are called _____, and they are often inaccurate and resistant to new information.

2. Discrimination is unjustifiable negative _____ toward a group. The terms "racism" and "_____" refer to institutional practices that discriminate even when there is no prejudicial intent.

3. Survey research suggests that racial prejudice in the United States has _____ since the early 1940s. While less blatant, prejudice exists in _____ forms and is also evident from experiments that have assessed people's actual _____ toward Blacks and Whites. Prejudiced attitudes and discriminatory behavior surface when they can hide behind the screen of some other _____.

4. While strong _____ stereotypes still exist, prejudice toward women has _____. For example, people no longer _____ women's work. However, as is true of racial prejudice, _____ gender prejudice still lives. Curiously, most women _____ feeling personally discriminated against.

SOCIAL SOURCES OF PREJUDICE

5. _____ status breeds prejudice as the group that enjoys superiority seeks to justify its standing. _____ is sometimes used to justify injustice and may explain why American church members are _____ racially prejudiced than nonmembers. However, faithful church attenders are _____ prejudiced than occasional attenders and the devout are _____ prejudiced than the nominally religious.

6. Prejudice can lead people to treat others in ways that trigger expected behavior, thus seeming to _____ the view one holds. Experiments also show that prejudice may arise from merely dividing people into _____. Even when the us-them distinction is trivial, people may still _____ their own group.

7. Once prejudice becomes a social norm, it is maintained partly through the inertia of _____. In addition, _____ supports, for example, segregation, schools, and the _____, may serve to bolster widespread prejudice

EMOTIONAL SOURCES OF PREJUDICE

8. _____ often evokes hostility, which may be vented on scapegoats. This phenomenon of "_____ aggression" may have contributed to lynchings of African Americans in the south after the Civil War. An important source of frustration is _____: One group's goal fulfillment becomes the other group's frustration.

9. One psychological benefit of prejudice is the feeling of _____ it provides and those who are low on the socioeconomic ladder tend to be

_____ prejudiced. The emotional needs that contribute to prejudice predominate in the _____ personality. Such persons tend to be prejudiced against all ethnic minorities.

COGNITIVE SOURCES OF PREJUDICE

10. Stereotyped beliefs are also by-products of our normal _____ processes. Once people are categorized into groups, we are likely to exaggerate the _____ within groups and the _____ between them. In viewing another group, we also tend to perceive that "they act and look alike, we don't."

11. _____ people draw our attention making us aware of differences we would otherwise not notice. We also better remember vivid cases and may use them to judge an entire _____. Our attentiveness to unusual occurrences can also create _____ correlations. For example, a minority person committing an unusual crime may lead us to associate such people with such behavior.

12. _____ errors can bias people's explanations of group members. In _____-_____ bias we explain away outgroup members' positive behaviors and attribute their negative behaviors to their dispositions. Blaming victims also results from believing the world is a _____ place in which people get what they deserve

13. By directing our _____ and memories, stereotypes lead us to find supporting evidence, even when none exists. Thus stereotypes are self-_____ When people get to know a person, they may set aside their stereotypes. Stereotypes are more potent when judging _____ individuals and when deciding policies regarding entire groups. Stereotypes can subtly color our assessments of individuals' behaviors, as when assertive behavior seems more _____ if coming from a woman.

MATCHING TERMS

Write the letter of the correct term from the right before the appropriate number on the left

_____ 1. Belief in the superiority of one's ethnic or cultural group.

_____ 2. Individuals' prejudicial attitudes and discriminatory behavior toward people of a given sex.

_____ 3. Unjustifiable negative behavior toward a group and its members.

_____ 4. Explaining away outgroup members' positive behaviors while attributing negative behaviors to their dispositions.

_____ 5. Institutional practices that subordinate people of a given race.

_____ 6. Tending toward punitiveness in thinking.

_____ 7. A negative prejudgment of a group and its members.

_____ 8. Forming a new stereotype of "professional, middle-class Blacks."

_____ 9. People deserve what they get.

_____ 10. An explanation for the lynchings of African-Americans in the South.

_____ 11. A belief about the personal attributes of a group of people.

_____ 12. Concern that one will be evaluated based on a negative stereotype.

_____ 13. Prejudice arises when groups compete for scarce resources.

_____ 14. Perceiving outgroup members as more similar to one another than are ingroup members.

a. outgroup homogeneity effect

b. realistic group conflict theory

c. authoritarianism

d. scapegoat theory

e. ethnocentrism

f. subtyping

g. stereotype threat

h. prejudice

i. discrimination

j. racism

k. stereotype

l. sexism

m. group-serving bias

n. the just world phenomenon

TRUE-FALSE REVIEW

Circle T if the statement is true and F if it is false.

T F 1. Prejudice is unjustifiable negative behavior toward a group and its members.

T F 2. Weight discrimination is notably greater than race or gender discrimination.

T F 3. More than 80 percent of Whites but only 40 percent of Blacks say race relations are generally good in their neighborhoods.

T F 4. Racism refers not only to attitudes but also to behavior and institutional practices that subordinate people of a given race.

T F 5. The phenomenon of greatest prejudice in the most intimate social realms seems to be universal.

T F 6. In a survey of students at 390 colleges and universities, more than half of African-American students felt excluded from social activities.

T F 7. In a national survey of Americans, more than half said they would be willing to "see a homosexual doctor."

T F 8. Strong gender stereotypes exist and members of the stereotyped group accept the stereotypes.

T F 9. Most women feel personally discriminated against.

T F 10. Half of African Americans perceive themselves as having faced discrimination within the last 30 days.

T F 11. Those for whom religion is an end in itself express less prejudice than those for whom religion is a means to an end.

T F 12. Some research indicates that merely composing groups X and Y with a flip of the coin is sufficient to produce ingroup bias.

T F 13. Children of employed women have less stereotyped views of men and women.

T F 14. Ingroup bias results as much or more from perceiving that one's own group is good as from a sense that other groups are bad.

T F 15. Compared to nonprejudiced people, prejudiced people take less time to categorize others by race.

T F 16. The authoritarian personality is prejudiced toward Blacks but not toward other minority groups.

T F 17. When White and Black students are shown faces of a few White and Black individuals and then asked to pick these individuals out of a photographic lineup, both White and Black students more accurately recognize the White faces than the Black.

T F 18. Black people in White cultures are slightly better than Whites at recognizing faces from another race.

T F 19. Teachers' stereotypes of motivational and achievement differences in students from different gender, ethnic, and class backgrounds have little basis in reality.

T F 20. Hate crimes have fluctuated with unemployment in recent decades.

T F 21. An emotion processing center in the brain becomes more active as a person views an unfamiliar person of another race.

T F 22. People often evaluate individuals more positively than the groups they compose.

T F 23. The need to believe in a just world provides an explanation for why we disparage victims of injustice.

T F 24. Recent research indicates that gender stereotypes seem to have very little effect on people's judgments of particular pieces of writing attributed to a man or to a woman.

T F 25. As African American students move from 8th to 10th grade, there is a weakening connection between their school performance and self-esteem.

MULTIPLE-CHOICE PRACTICE TEST

Circle the correct letter.

1. Prejudice is a negative _____ while discrimination is negative _____.

   a. belief; feeling
   b. generalization; practice
   c. attitude; behavior
   d. stereotype; practice

2. Stereotypes are to discrimination as _____ are to _____.

   a. categories; feelings
   b. attitudes; actions
   c. emotions; practice
   d. beliefs; behavior

144

3. Racism
   a. can refer to institutional practices that discriminate even when there is no prejudicial intent
   b. refers to institutional practices that discriminate but only if there is prejudicial intent
   c. refers only to individuals' prejudicial attitudes
   d. refers only to individuals' discriminatory behavior

4. Survey research on racial prejudice in the United States indicates that
   a. racial prejudice has increased since the 1980s
   b. racial prejudice increased from the 1950s to 1970s but has decreased since then
   c. racial prejudice has plummeted since the 1940s
   d. the level of racial prejudice has remained unchanged since 1952

5. When Claude Steele and his colleagues gave a very difficult math test to men and women students and said that women usually underperformed men on the test, the women
   a. outperformed the men
   b. did in fact perform more poorly than the men
   c. performed as well as the men
   d. with more liberal attitudes outperformed the women with more conservative attitudes

6. Which of the following is true?
   a. strong gender stereotypes continue to exist
   b. prejudice against women has not declined in the last 15 years
   c. racial stereotypes are stronger than gender stereotypes
   d. stereotypes are the same as prejudices

7. Most Americans agree that
   a. the activities of married women are best confined to the home and family
   b. they would probably move if Black people came to live in great numbers in their neighborhood
   c. the two sexes are equally emotional
   d. they would vote for a qualified woman whom their party nominated for president

8. When visitors to the University of British Columbia were asked to indicate which traits described themselves, males were _____ more likely than females to describe themselves as assertive and dominant, and were _____ less likely to describe themselves as tender and compassionate.
   a. slightly; slightly
   b. two times; two times
   c. slightly; two times
   d. two times; slightly

9. In the 1950s, racial integration was accepted in Indiana steel mills and West Virginia coal mines. However, in the neighborhoods of those employed in the mills and mines, segregation was practiced. This is an example of how prejudice may be based in

   a. authoritarianism
   b. the just world phenomenon
   c. frustration
   d. conformity

10. The in-group bias seems to occur more frequently among

   a. females than among males
   b. the young than among the old
   c. people from individualistic cultures than among people from communal cultures
   d. Blacks than among Whites

11. Which best summarizes the research findings on people's evaluations of work attributed to women or to men?

   a. people's judgments of someone's work are not significantly affected by whether the work is attributed to a male or a female
   b. both males and females show a tendency to deprecate women's work
   c. males show a tendency to deprecate women's work while females' judgments are not affected by whether the work is attributed to a male or female
   d. females but not males show a tendency to deprecate women's work

12. The most recent explanation which social psychologists have offered for prejudice emphasizes _____ sources.

   a. social
   b. cognitive
   c. emotional
   d. political

13. The tendency for more lynchings to occur in years when cotton prices were low was cited in the text as evidence for

   a. the just world phenomenon
   b. the ultimate attribution error
   c. the scapegoat theory
   d. psychoanalytic theory

14. Realistic group conflict theory suggests that prejudice arises

   a. where there is a long history of distrust between two groups
   b. when a new group moves into an area
   c. when groups fail to communicate clearly with each other
   d. when groups compete for scarce resources

15. Research indicates that those professing traditional Christian beliefs are _____ than those with less traditional beliefs.

    a. less racially prejudiced
    b. more racially prejudiced
    c. less authoritarian
    d. less racially prejudiced but more prejudiced toward women

16. Studies by Pettigrew of Whites in South Africa and the American South revealed that during the 1950s

    a. prejudice had its basis in competition for housing and jobs
    b. those who were prejudiced were authoritarian personalities
    c. prejudice was based in displaced aggression
    d. those who conformed most to other social norms were also most prejudiced

17. The idea that we find it useful to put people, ourselves included, into categories is an important assumption of _____ theory.

    a. just world
    b. realistic group conflict
    c. social identity
    d. cognitive bias

18. Which of the following is particularly characteristic of the authoritarian personality?

    a. being intolerant of weakness
    b. experiencing a happy childhood
    c. occupying a political office with considerable authority
    d. being an only child

19. The "personal/group discrimination discrepancy" refers to the finding that

    a. individuals deny being personally discriminated against but see their groups as victims
    b. individuals believe they are personally disciminated against but not their groups
    c. many people show prejudice toward individuals but not toward their groups
    d. many people show prejudice toward groups but not toward their individual members

20. In repressive regimes across the world, people who become torturers tend to have

    a. low self-esteem
    b. authoritarian attitudes
    c. low intelligence
    d. a sense of external control

21. Research investigating the effects of moods on stereotyping indicates that

    a. bad moods amplify outgroup stereotyping while good moods decrease it
    b. positive emotions improve complex thinking and thus the ability to see individual differences
    c. bad moods lead to more introspective thinking and thus less stereotyping
    d. feeling really good may prime feelings of superiority

22. The group-serving bias seems to be less characteristic of groups that stress

    a. individualism
    b. honesty
    c. modesty
    d. intelligence

23. The stereotype of _____ is held by both men and women, by both feminists and nonfeminists.

    a. men as leaders
    b. men as decision makers
    c. women as homemakers
    d. women as mediators

24. According to the text, the authoritarian personality is an example of

    a. how conformity supports prejudice
    b. a cognitive source of prejudice
    c. how emotional needs contribute to prejudice
    d. how social inequalities breed prejudice

25. The co-occurrence of two distinctive events can create

    a. belief in a just world
    b. illusory correlation
    c. illusion of control
    d. the ultimate attribution error

26. Students were told the actions of 50 men, 10 of whom had performed either nonviolent crimes or violent crimes. When later asked to make judgments about the men,

    a. the subjects shown the list with the violent crimes most overestimated the number of criminal acts
    b. the subjects shown the list with the nonviolent crimes most overestimated the number of criminal acts
    c. the subjects judged all the men to be members of outgroups
    d. male subjects made more accurate judgments about the number of criminal acts than did female subjects

27. In one study, students were told that various members of "Group A" or "Group B" did either something desirable or something undesirable. While many more statements described members of Group A than Group B, both groups were associated with nine desirable behaviors for every four undesirable behaviors. Results indicated

   a. that students perceived members of Group B more negatively
   b. that students perceived members of Group A more negatively
   c. no differences in the students' perceptions of the groups
   d. that "authoritarian" students viewed Group A more negatively

28. Researchers who used a uniform strategy to negotiate the lowest price on a new car found that _____ were offered the highest, or worst, price.

   a. White males
   b. Black males
   c. White females
   d. Black females

29. A study of photographs in magazines and newspapers revealed that prominence was given to

   a. men's faces and women's bodies
   b. men's bodies and women's faces
   c. Whites' faces and Blacks' bodies
   d. Whites' bodies and Blacks' faces

30. John Williams and his colleagues found that people everywhere perceive women as more _____, and men as more _____.

   a. outgoing; reserved
   b. agreeable; outgoing
   c. depressed; contented
   d. talkative; disagreeable

31. According to Lerner, our need to believe in a just world often leads us to blame

   a. fate
   b. supernatural forces
   c. the social structure
   d. the victim

32. According to the text, stereotypes are resistant to change because

   a. for the most part, they are accurate reflections of reality
   b. our prejudgments influence how we interpret and process information
   c. they are always based in an authoritarian attitude which is blind to disconfirming evidence
   d. they are held by people with low intelligence

33. Mr. Watson's belief that Blacks are lazy is an example of _____.
His refusal to rent an apartment to a Black family is an example of _____

a. a stereotype; sexism
b. discrimination; prejudice
c. a stereotype; discrimination
d. racism; prejudice

34. Forming a new stereotype of "serious, college-bound young people" to protect one's larger negative stereotype of irresponsible teenagers is an example of

a. just world thinking
b. authoritarianism
c. subtyping
d. external attribution

35. Which of the following would you not expect to be true of the authoritarian personality?

a. to discriminate against American Indians
b. to want to achieve high social status
c. to be respectful of police
d. to be opposed to capital punishment

36. Which of the following would be an example of the "group-serving bias"?

a. Veryl believes that women are unemployed because of discrimination while men are unemployed because of low motivation
b. Sue believes that members of her own family are prejudiced while her husband's family is tolerant
c. Chuck believes that mistakes made by both men and women are due to low intelligence
d. Bill believes that groups outperform individuals in solving problems

37. The just world phenomenon may lead us to believe that an unemployed person is

a. a victim of discrimination
b. lazy
c. in need of sympathy
d. in need of a retraining program

38. John has just failed a chemistry test. He goes back to his apartment and criticizes his roommate's choice of music. What term best describes John's behavior?

a. institutionalized aggression
b. just world action
c. displaced aggression
d. authoritarian regression

39. Which of the following would be an example of racism as the term is defined in the text?

a. Mr. Jones' refusal to rent his apartments to Chinese
b. Mrs. Smith's prejudice toward Hispanics
c. a government regulation that prevents inner-city residents from being recruited to serve as Army officers
d. all of the above

40. The results of one social-psychological study indicated that observers who discovered that a fellow worker had received a large prize as the result of a random drawing subsequently concluded that he had in fact worked especially hard. This is an example of

a. vivid, anecdotal information being more important than base-rate data
b. disguised hostility
c. outgroup bias
d. just world phenomenon

SHORT ESSAY QUESTIONS

Answer the following questions in the space provided.

1. Distinguish between prejudice, discrimination, and racism.

2. What evidence indicates that racial prejudice still exists in the United States?

3. What evidence suggests that gender prejudice is declining?

4. Explain how unequal status breeds prejudice.

5. What is the relationship between religion and prejudice?

6. Describe two institutional supports for prejudice.

7. Identify characteristics of the authoritarian personality

8. What is meant by the term "just world phenomenon"?

9. Describe two ways in which our normal thinking processes may be a source of prejudice

ANSWER KEY

Chapter Review

1. prejudgment
   stereotypes

2. behavior
   sexism

3. declined
   subtle
   behavior
   motive

4. gender
   declined
   deprecate
   subtle
   deny

5. Unequal
   Religion
   more
   less
   less

6. confirm
   groups
   favor

7. conformity

   institutional
   media

8. Frustration
   displaced
   competition

9. superiority
   more
   authoritarian

10. thinking
    similarities
    differences

11. Distinctive
    group
    illusory

12. Attribution
    group-serving
    just

13. interpretations
    perpetuating
    unknown
    aggressive

Matching Terms

1.	e	8.	f
2.	l	9.	n
3.	i	10.	d
4.	m	11.	k
5.	j	12.	g
6.	c	13.	b
7.	h	14.	a

True-False Review

1.	F	14.	T
2.	T	15.	F
3.	F	16.	F
4.	T	17.	F
5.	T	18.	T
6.	T	19.	F
7.	F	20.	F
8.	T	21.	T
9.	F	22.	T
10.	T	23.	T
11.	T	24.	T
12.	T	25.	T
13.	T		

Multiple-Choice Practice Test

1.	c	21.	d
2.	d	22.	c
3.	a	23.	a
4.	c	24.	c
5.	b	25.	b
6.	a	26.	a
7.	d	27.	a
8.	a	28.	d
9.	d	29.	a
10.	c	30.	b
11.	a	31.	d
12.	b	32.	b
13.	c	33.	c
14.	d	34.	c
15.	b	35.	d
16.	d	36.	a
17.	c	37.	b
18.	a	38.	c
19.	a	39.	d
20.	b	40.	d

CHAPTER 10

AGGRESSION: HURTING OTHERS

CHAPTER OBJECTIVES

After completing your study of this chapter you should be able to:

1. Define aggression and explain the difference between hostile and instrumental aggression.

2. Discuss the instinct view of aggression.

3. Describe biological influences on aggression.

4. Identify the causes and consequences of frustration.

5. Discuss the social learning view of aggression.

6. Identify conditions that tend to provoke aggression.

7. Describe the effects of viewing pornography.

8. Describe television's effects on thinking and behavior.

9. Discuss ways of reducing aggression.

CHAPTER REVIEW

Supply the words necessary to complete each of the following statements.

WHAT IS AGGRESSION?

1. Aggression is physical or verbal behavior intended to _____ someone. _____ aggression springs from anger and aims to

injure. _____ aggression also aims to hurt but only as a means to an end.

THEORIES OF AGGRESSION

2. Sigmund Freud and Konrad Lorenz argued that aggression is _____. In contrast to Freud, Lorenz saw aggression as _____ rather than self-destructive. Both Freud and Lorenz agreed that if aggressive energy is not discharged it builds up until it _____.

3. Although the evidence does not support the instinct view, research has identified _____ influences upon aggression including _____ systems, heredity, and blood _____.

4. A second theory, proposed by John Dollard and his associates in 1939, is that _____, or the blocking of goal-directed behavior, invariably leads to aggression. Leonard Berkowitz, in a revision of the theory, states that frustration produces _____, an emotional readiness to aggress. A frustrated person is especially likely to lash out when aggressive _____ pull the cork.

5. Frustration is created by a gap between our _____ and our attainments. _____ deprivation is the perception that we are less well off than others to whom we compare ourselves.

6. _____ learning theory presents aggression as learned behavior. Through experience and by _____ others' success we learn that aggression often pays. Albert Bandura contends that aggressive acts are most likely when we are _____ by aversive experiences and it seems safe and _____ to aggress.

INFLUENCES ON AGGRESSION

7. Animals' reactions to shock indicate that _____ may provoke aggressive acts. Temporary climate variations affect one's behavior, and _____ has been shown to increase aggression. Being _____ by another and crowding are also conducive to aggression.

8. Research indicates that our experience of emotion depends on how we _____ our bodily states. Thus arousal from almost any source, even physical _____ or sexual stimulation, can be interpreted as _____ and lead to aggression. Recent studies indicate that viewing pornography distorts _____ of sexual reality, and may contribute to men's _____ toward women. Rather than advocate censorship, many psychologists favor "_____ _____ training."

9. The _____ hypothesis suggests that viewing violent drama enables people to release pent-up hostility. Research indicates that viewing violence produces an _____ in aggressive behavior especially in people who are provoked. It seems also to _____ viewers to aggression and to alter their _____ of reality. Television's greatest effect may be indirect as it _____ other activities.

10. Circumstances that provoke individuals to aggress can provoke _____ to do likewise. In fact, social interaction can actually _____ the aggressive reactions of individuals.

REDUCING AGGRESSION

11. The catharsis hypothesis which predicts that the aggressive drive will be _____ after one releases aggressive energy has not been confirmed. In some studies aggressing has actually led to _____ aggression.

12. Social learning theory proposes we reduce aggression by reducing _____ stimulation and by _____ and modeling cooperative, nonaggressive behavior. _____ is considerably less effective because it provides aversive stimulation and models the very behavior it seeks to prevent.

13. Since aggression is increased in the presence of aggressive cues, limiting the availability of _____ can reduce violence.

MATCHING TERMS

Write the letter of the correct term from the right before the appropriate number on the left.

_____ 1. Redirecting aggression to a safer target.

_____ 2. The blocking of goal-directed behavior.

_____ 3. Innate, unlearned behavior exhibited by all members of a species.

_____ 4. An author of frustration-aggression theory.

_____ 5. It springs from anger and its goal is to injure.

_____ 6. Many psychologists favor this as an alternative to censorship.

_____ 7. Positive, helpful social behavior.

_____ 8. A perspective that emphasizes the importance of modeling.

_____ 9. It aims to hurt but only as a means to some other end.

_____ 10. The feeling of not having enough space.

_____ 11. Stated that a primitive death urge accounts for aggression.

_____ 12. Our feeling that we are less well off than others to whom we compare ourselves.

_____ 13. The leading proponent of social learning theory.

_____ 14. Emotional release.

a. hostile aggression

b. prosocial behavior

c. relative deprivation

d. catharsis

e. displacement

f. crowding

g. media awareness training

h. social learning theory

i. frustration

j. Dollard

k. Freud

l. Bandura

m. instinctive behavior

n. instrumental aggression

TRUE-FALSE REVIEW

Circle T if the statement is true and F if it is false.

T F   1. Aggression is any behavior that results in harm coming to another person.

T F   2. All psychologists agree that aggression is maladaptive and self-destructive.

T F   3. Hostile aggression seeks to injure but only as a means to some other end.

T F   4. Sigmund Freud theorized that human nature has within it a primitive death urge.

T F   5. Violent people are more likely to consume alcohol and to become aggressive when intoxicated.

T F   6. The catharsis hypothesis assumes that aggression is produced by frustration.

T F   7. Half of identical twins of convicted criminals also have criminal records.

T F   8. In 65 percent of homicides, the murderer and/or the victim had been drinking.

T F   9. Animals of many species have been bred for aggressiveness.

T F   10. Research indicates that 70 percent of juveniles in detention did not grow up with two parents.

T F   11. Revolutions of rising expectations indicate that those who are the most deprived are also those most frustrated.

T F   12. The term "relative deprivation" refers to the tendency to adapt to a given level of stimulation and thus to react to changes from that level.

T F   13. After a big basketball game between archrivals, testosterone levels rose in the winning fans and fell in the losing fans.

T F   14. Social learning theory denies that frustration plays any role in aggression.

T F   15. When Washington, D.C., adopted a law restricting handgun possession, the number of gun-related murders and suicides dropped about 25 percent.

T F   16. Research has indicated that violent acts are more likely to occur on hot days.

T F   17. Half of the respondents in one survey of college women report having suffered some form of sexual assault on a date.

T F 18. The Surgeon General has concluded that television and pornography are the primary causes of social violence.

T F 19. Most abused children eventually become abusive parents.

T F 20. In one survey of prison inmates, 4 out of 10 said they had attempted specific crimes they had seen on television.

T F 21. Correlational studies but not laboratory experiments indicate that viewing aggression leads to aggression.

T F 22. Viewing television can mold our conceptions of the real world.

T F 23. After a war, a nation's murder rate tends to jump.

T F 24. High levels of serotonin are often found among violence-prone children and adults.

T F 25. Reward for nonaggression is more effective than punishment for aggression in reducing violence.

MULTIPLE-CHOICE PRACTICE TEST

Circle the correct letter.

1. According to the text, aggression always

   a. causes physical pain
   b. involves intent to harm someone
   c. involves emotional arousal
   d. is committed by someone who has been deliberately provoked

2. The murders committed by mobster "hit men" provide an example of

   a. emotional aggression
   b. silent aggression
   c. how catharsis can reduce aggression
   d. instrumental aggression

3. Research on biological influences on aggression indicates that

   a. animals of many species can be bred for aggressiveness
   b. neural influences facilitate animal aggression but not human aggression
   c. human aggression is instinctive
   d. there are no biochemical influences on aggression in humans

4. In contrast to Freud's view of aggression, Lorenz

   a. supports the social learning explanation for aggression
   b. views aggression as instinctive
   c. views aggression as adaptive rather than destructive
   d. does not believe we have innate mechanisms for inhibiting aggression

5. Which of the following is false?

   a. animals' "social" aggression and "silent" aggression seem to involve the same brain region
   b. alcohol enhances violence by reducing people's self-awareness
   c. low levels of serotonin are often found in the violence-prone
   d. "hostile" aggression springs from emotions such as anger

6. Research on the effects of televised violence indicates that

   a. viewing violence produces a modest increase in aggression
   b. viewing violence produces catharsis and thus a reduction in aggression
   c. there is no relationship between viewing aggression and behaving aggressively
   d. viewing violence increases aggression in adolescents but not in children

7. What criticism has been leveled against instinct theory as an explanation for human aggression?

   a. it is an example of naming social behavior but not explaining it
   b. research has indicated no clear biological influences on aggression
   c. it necessarily implies that aggression is adaptive
   d. it misinterprets correlation as evidence for causation

8. Compared to prisoners convicted of nonviolent crimes, those convicted of unprovoked violent crimes tend to

   a. be first-borns
   b. have authoritarian attitudes
   c. be older
   d. have higher testosterone levels

9. The text suggests that one reason Vancouver, British Columbia, has a 40 percent lower overall murder rate than Seattle, Washington, is because Vancouver

   a. has a lower average temperature
   b. has a lower unemployment rate
   c. restricts handgun ownership
   d. has a less congested population

10. In brain scans of men with antisocial conduct disorder, Adrian Raine and his colleagues found that the _____ was _____ than normal.

    a. prefrontal cortex; smaller
    b. prefrontal cortex; larger
    c. amydala; smaller
    d. amydala; larger

11. Research on rape in the U.S. suggests that

    a. nine in 10 stranger rapes are not reported to police
    b. at least 25 percent of women surveyed reported an experience that met the legal definition of rape or attempted rape
    c. today's young women are less likely to report having been raped than are older women
    d. the rape rate is lower than in most other industrialized countries

12. In a revision of frustration-aggression theory, Berkowitz theorized that

    a. frustration produces escape more often than aggression
    b. aggression is learned through a modeling effect
    c. aggressive cues can release bottled-up anger
    d. frustration is instinctive

13. To know whether people are frustrated we need to know

    a. their expectations and their attainments
    b. their level of deprivation and their power
    c. their wants and their intelligence
    d. their needs and their age

14. In a study of more than 200,000 Californians who bought handguns, _____ was the leading cause of death in the following year.

    a. heart attack
    b. accidental shooting
    c. murder
    d. suicide

15. Emotional arousal plus anticipated consequences provides the formula for aggression according to

    a. ethological theory
    b. catharsis theory
    c. frustration-aggression theory
    d. social learning theory

16. According to Bandura, a social learning theorist,

    a. frustration plays no role in aggression
    b. observing aggressive models promotes aggression
    c. the hydraulic model offers the best explanation for aggression
    d. hostile aggression is instinctive and instrumental aggression is learned

17. In studying the capacity of electric shock to elicit attack behavior in rats, Nathan Azrin and his colleagues found that

a. the shocked animals were choosy about their attack targets and would only attack other animals of the same species
b. increasing the shock resulted in attempts on the part of the rats to escape rather than to attack
c. the shock-attack reaction was clearly present in many different species
d. shocks alone and not other aversive stimuli elicited attack

18. Which of the following is false?

a. pain heightens aggressiveness in animals but not in humans
b. being insulted by another is especially conducive to aggression
c. in laboratory experiments heat triggers retaliative actions
d. according to social learning theory, aggression is most likely when we are aroused and it seems safe and rewarding to aggress

19. In the Schacter and Singer experiment, which subjects felt the most anger?

a. those who were given an adrenaline injection, were forewarned of the drug's effects, and were in the company of a euphoric person
b. those who were given an adrenaline injection, were not forewarned of the drug's effects, and were in the company of a euphoric person
c. those who were given an adrenaline injection, were forewarned of the drug's effects, and were in the company of a hostile person
d. those who were given an adrenaline injection, were not forewarned of the drug's effects, and were in the company of a hostile person

20. Living three to a room in a college dorm seems to

a. diminish one's sense of control
b. lead to the establishment of stronger friendships
c. lead to more hostile but less instrumental aggression
d. improve grades because students are more likely to study in the library

21. When college males have been asked whether there was any chance they would rape a woman "if you could be assured that no one would know and that you could in no way be punished," about _____ admit to at least a slim possibility of doing so.

a. 1 in 20
b. 1 in 10

c. 1 in 5
d. 1 in 3

22. According to the author of the text, television's most influential effect may be that it

   a. desensitizes people to violence around them
   b. is the major cause of social violence
   c. presents an unreal picture of the world
   d. replaces other activities that people might engage in

23. Correlational research indicates that as pornography has become more widely available, the rate of reported rape has

   a. increased
   b. decreased
   c. remained unchanged
   d. increased in the short run but decreased in the long run

24. According to the text, the fact that people from Hong Kong feel more fearful on their city streets that do people from Toronto may be due to the fact that Hong Kong

   a. has a higher average temperature
   b. has a lower per capita income
   c. has a higher crime rate
   d. is more densely populated

25. Sales rates of sexually explicit magazines such as Hustler and Playboy were positively correlated with state

   a. rape rates
   b. unemployment rates
   c. divorce rates
   d. child abuse rates

26. In examining the relationship between viewing violence and aggressiveness in boys, Eron and Huesmann found that

   a. the viewing of violence at age eight was negatively correlated with aggressiveness at age nineteen
   b. the viewing of violence at age eight was positively correlated with aggressiveness at age nineteen
   c. aggressiveness at age eight was positively correlated with the viewing of violence at age nineteen
   d. both b and c are true

27. Within the United States, Southerners are more likely to advocate

   a. violence that protects one's property
   b. all forms of violence
   c. stricter gun control legislation
   d. media awareness training

28. Research indicates that in comparison to light viewers, heavy viewers of television

   a. engage in greater prosocial behavior
   b. underestimate the number of murders that occur annually in the United States
   c. think the world is a more dangerous place
   d. tend to be more extraverted

29. Which of the following is true of findings regarding the catharsis hypothesis?

   a. catharsis never occurs
   b. the calming effect of retaliation seems to occur only in very specific circumstances
   c. the catharsis hypothesis has been well-supported
   d. the catharsis hypothesis is valid for adults but not for children

30. Violent pornographic films often convey a false impression that

   a. women enjoy aggressive sexual encounters
   b. women are more likely to be rape victims than are men
   c. most rapes are never reported to the police
   d. most rapes are committed by victims' dates or acquaintances

31. According to the text, the statement to a friend, "When you talk like that I feel irritated,"

   a. is, by definition, an act of angry aggression
   b. is best unsaid for it will prove frustrating to the friend and invite retaliation
   c. provides an informative, nonaggressive expression of feeling
   d. is best unsaid for while it may prove cathartic for you in the short run, it will make you feel more aggressive in the long run

32. The text suggests that crime rates may be higher in communities and nations with large income inequality because of

   a. catharsis   c. crowding
   b. displacement   d. relative deprivation

33. University men who were angered by a fellow student retaliated with much stronger shock

   a. when in groups than when alone
   b. when the experimenter was not present than when he was observing their aggression
   c. when the subject was an acquaintance than when he was a stranger
   d. if after being angered, but before delivering shock, they were exposed to mildly erotic stimuli

34. Which of the following is probably least effective in reducing aggression?

    a. rewards for nonaggressive behavior
    b. reducing the availability of weapons
    c. ignoring aggressive behavior
    d. punishing aggressive behavior

35. Which of the following would be an example of aggression as defined in the text?

    a. a wife deliberately belittles her husband in front of friends after he burns the pot roast
    b. a golfer accidentally hits another player with a golf ball
    c. a nurse gives a penicillin shot to a child
    d. a salesman tops his previous record by selling 50 cars in one month

36. A person kicking a cat after losing a game of checkers is an example of

    a. regression   c. relative frustration
    b. displacement   d. the weapons effect

37. Cedric and Phillip are college roommates who spend many hours each week playing violent video games. Research suggests that, compared to their peers, Cedric and Phillip are likely to

    a. be less physically aggressive   c. be more physically aggressive
    b. have lower levels of testosterone d. have higher levels of testosterone

38. John has just received a 5 percent increase in salary. However, after learning that his coworkers have all received 10 percent increases, John becomes angry with his employer. We can understand John's feelings in terms of

    a. relative deprivation
    b. displacement
    c. Parkinson's second law
    d. the hydraulic model of aggression

39. As part of therapy, a clinical psychologist encourages her patients to install a punching bag in their homes to release hostility. The therapist apparently believes in

    a. social learning theory   c. the catharsis hypothesis
    b. Parkinson's second law   d. the adaptation-level phenomenon

40. Which of the following is the best example of instrumental aggression?

    a. an angry football player tackles a quarterback after he has completed a long pass
    b. a jealous wife finds her husband with another woman and shoots both of them
    c. a group of former soldiers kill the dictator of a small country for $10,000
    d. a man smashes his television set after he finds it does not work

SHORT ESSAY QUESTIONS

Answer the following questions in the space provided.

1. State the difference between hostile and instrumental aggression.

2. Discuss how aggression is biologically influenced.

3. Give an example of relative deprivation from your own life.

4. Briefly describe the social learning view of aggression.

5. Describe three aversive experiences that may heighten aggression

6. Explain how any form of emotional arousal can produce anger

7. List two effects of viewing pornography.

8. Describe the effects of television's portrayal of violence.

9. List three effective ways of reducing aggression.

ANSWER KEY

Chapter Review

1. hurt
   Hostile
   Instrumental

2. instinctual
   adaptive
   explodes

3. biological
   neural
   chemistry

4. frustration
   anger
   cues

5. expectations
   relative

6. Social
   observing
   aroused
   rewarding

7. pain
   heat
   attacked

8. interpret
   exercise
   anger
   perceptions
   aggression
   media awareness

9. catharsis
   increase
   desensitize
   conception
   replaces

10. groups
    amplify

11. reduced
    heightened

12. aversive
    rewarding
    Punishment

13. weapons

Matching Terms

1. e
2. i
3. m
4. j
5. a
6. g
7. b
8. h
9. n
10. f
11. k
12. c
13. l
14. d

True-False Review

1.	F	14.	F
2.	F	15.	T
3.	F	16.	T
4.	T	17.	T
5.	T	18.	F
6.	F	19.	F
7.	T	20.	T
8.	T	21.	F
9.	T	22.	T
10.	T	23.	T
11.	F	24.	F
12.	F	25.	T
13.	T		

Multiple-Choice Practice Test

1.	b	21.	d
2.	d	22.	d
3.	a	23.	a
4.	c	24.	d
5.	a	25.	a
6.	a	26.	b
7.	a	27.	a
8.	d	28.	c
9.	c	29.	b
10.	a	30.	a
11.	b	31.	c
12.	c	32.	d
13.	a	33.	a
14.	d	34.	d
15.	d	35.	a
16.	b	36.	b
17.	c	37.	c
18.	a	38.	a
19.	d	39.	c
20.	a	40.	c

CHAPTER 11

ATTRACTION AND INTIMACY: LIKING AND LOVING OTHERS

<u>CHAPTER OBJECTIVES</u>

After completing your study of this chapter you should be able to:

1. Discuss the role of proximity and physical attractiveness in initial attraction.

2. Discuss research findings on the role of similarity in friendship and describe how liking is usually mutual.

3. Explain the reward theory of attraction.

4. Describe the nature of passionate love and identify cultural, personality, and gender variations in love.

5. Discuss the nature of companionate love.

6. Identify the different attachment styles that characterize interpersonal relationships.

7. Discuss the importance of equity and self-disclosure in close relationships.

8. Identify several predictors of a stable marriage and describe the detachment process.

<u>CHAPTER REVIEW</u>

Supply the words necessary to complete each of the following statements.

1. We have an intense need to _____, that is, to connect to others in enduring close relationships.

FRIENDSHIPS

2. A powerful predictor of whether any two people are friends is their sheer _____ to one another. It provides people with the opportunity for _____ and thus to discover their similarities and to feel one another's liking. Even the _____ of interacting with another can boost liking. Research also indicates that mere repeated _____ tends to increase attraction.

3. A second determinant of one's initial liking for another is physical _____. The _____ phenomenon is the tendency for people to pair off with others who are about as attractive as themselves. Research indicates the presence of a strong physical-attractiveness _____: the assumption that what is beautiful is _____. Evolutionary psychologists suggest that males prefer female characteristics that signify _____ capacity. Females prefer males who have high _____.

4. Acquaintances are likely to develop a friendship if there is _____ of beliefs, attitudes, and values. Little support has been found for the _____ hypothesis which proposes that we are attracted to those whose needs are different from our own. Apparently _____ rarely attract.

5. We are also likely to develop friendships with people who _____ us This is particularly true when we do not attribute the other's flattery to some ingratiating motive, when we have recently been deprived of _____, and when the other's praise _____ earlier criticism.

6. We like those who _____ us or those who are associated with _____ feelings.

LOVE

7. Robert Sternberg views love as a triangle whose three sides are _____, intimacy, and _____.

8. _____ love is a state of intense longing for union with another. Such love often includes both elation and gloom, exhilaration and misery.

9. The two-factor theory of emotion states that arousal x _____ = emotion. Thus any arousal can intensify passionate feelings provided one can attribute some of the arousal to a _____ stimulus.

10. Most cultures do have a concept of _____ love. But in some cultures, notably those practicing arranged marriages, love tends to _____ marriage

Studies of men and women have also found that _____ tend to fall in love more readily.

11. _____ love is the affection we feel for those with whom our lives are deeply intertwined. Such love thrives where a relationship is _____ and mutually rewarding.

MAINTAINING CLOSE RELATIONSHIPS

12. From infancy to old age, _____ are central to human life. In terms of specific style, _____ individuals find it easy to get close to others. _____-ambivalent individuals are less trusting, and thus more possessive and jealous. _____ individuals may fear closeness or want to feel self-sufficient.

13. We exchange rewards by an _____ principle. It states that what people receive from a relationship should be _____ to what they contribute to it. Tit-for-tat exchanges seem to increase people's liking for one another when their relationship is relatively _____ but diminish liking when the two seek true _____. Still, relationships are likely to endure when both partners feel it to be equitable.

14. Intimacy is fostered by reciprocal _____ in which we drop our masks and gradually let ourselves be known as we are. Couples who most reveal themselves to one another tend to express _____ satisfaction with their relationship.

ENDING RELATIONSHIPS

15. Divorce risk is lower for those who marry after age _____, are well-_____, and are _____ committed. As an alternative to divorce, some people cope with a failing relationship by exhibiting _____, optimistically waiting for conditions to improve. Others passively allow the relationship to deteriorate. Still others _____ their concerns and take active steps to improve the relationship.

MATCHING TERMS

Write the letter of the correct term from the right before the appropriate number on the left.

_____ 1. A strategy to gain another's favor.

_____ 2. A need to connect with others in enduring, close relationships.

_____ 3. Stimuli are rated more positively after being shown repeatedly.

_____ 4. Liking those who are associated with good feelings.

_____ 5. What is beautiful is good.

_____ 6. This fosters intimacy.

_____ 7. Outcomes are in proportion to inputs.

_____ 8. The affection we feel for those with whom our lives are deeply intertwined.

_____ 9. One of the most powerful predictors of whether two people are friends.

_____ 10. People choose partners who are about as attractive as themselves.

_____ 11. "Intense longing for union with another."

_____ 12. People attract those whose needs are different, in ways that complement their own.

a. equity

b. proximity

c. mere-exposure effect

d. physical-attractiveness stereotype

e. matching phenomenon

f. complementarity hypothesis

g. ingratiation

h. reward principle

i. passionate love

j. self-disclosure

k. companionate love

l. need to belong

TRUE-FALSE REVIEW

Circle T if the statement is true and F if it is false.

T F   1. Merely anticipating that we will interact with someone increases liking of that person

T F   2. The happiest couples are those who idealize one another, even seeing their partners more positively than their partners see themselves.

T F   3. Cognitive dissonance theory provides the most popular theory of social attraction.

T F   4. Equity is a condition in which people receive equal outcomes from a relationship.

T F   5. One experiment found that tit-for-tat exchanges actually diminished liking when two people sought true friendship.

T F   6. College students who evaluated strangers in a pleasant room liked them better than did those who did their evaluations in an uncomfortably hot room.

T F   7. One of the most powerful predictors of whether any two people are friends is their sheer proximity to one another.

T F   8. Novel stimuli are rated more negatively after being shown repeatedly.

T F   9. Voters on the losing side of an election find that their opinion of the winning candidate becomes increasingly worse.

T F   10. Physically attractive men and women tend to be looked on by others as colder, dumber, and less moral than plainer people.

T F   11. Destructive acts harm relationships more than constructive acts build them.

T F   12. Women tend to be judged as more physically attractive if they have "baby-face" features that suggest nondominance.

T F   13. A 17-year-old girl's facial attractiveness is a weak predictor of her attractiveness at age 30.

T F   14. Months or years later, people recall more pain over spurning someone's love than over having been spurned.

T F   15. Evidence strongly supports the complementarity hypothesis.

T F   16. We are more attracted to someone who likes us from the start than to someone who likes us after initially disliking us.

T F 17. Across the world people show little agreement about the features of an ideal male or female face.

T F 18. In experiments, people who are left out of a simple game of ball tossing feel deflated and stressed.

T F 19. Men are more likely than women to initiate the breakup of a premarital romance.

T F 20. Bad moods affect our thinking and memory more than do good moods.

T F 21. Those who do exciting things together report the best relationships.

T F 22. Only 4 in 10 infants exhibit secure attachment.

T F 23. The two-factor theory of emotion states that love is a product of jealousy and ecstasy.

T F 24. Researchers have found that women are often more willing to disclose their fears and weaknesses than are men.

T F 25. People who live in a small town or on a farm are less likely to divorce.

MULTIPLE-CHOICE PRACTICE TEST

Circle the correct letter.

1. The need to belong and to form close interpersonal relationships

   a. is at the core of our existence and thus is characteristic of people everywhere
   b. is largely a 20th century motive that is most evident in industrialized societies
   c. is a learned motive serving our more fundamental need for self-esteem
   d. conflicts with our more basic need to survive

2. The concept of romantic love is present

   a. only in individualistic societies
   b. only in affluent societies
   c. only in cultures where there are clear differences in gender roles
   d. in most cultures

3. In his studies of ostracism, Kipling Williams found that

   a. even experiencing "cyber-ostracism" by faceless people whom one will never meet has a negative impact
   b. ostracism has a negative impact only if one feels excluded by family or close friends
   c. being excluded has no effect on people of high status
   d. only people in western cultures use acts of ostracism to regulate social behavior

4. Our desire to return a favor received from another is best explained in terms of the

   a. complementarity hypothesis
   b. equity rule
   c. matching phenomenon
   d. mere-exposure effect

5. Reward theory states that

   a. rewards foster romantic but not companionate love
   b. companionate love is fostered by long periods of separation
   c. flattery always leads to increased liking
   d. we like those people who are associated with good feelings

6. Which of the following is supported by the research on social attraction?

   a. familiarity breeds fondness
   b. opposites attract
   c. beauty times brains equals a constant
   d. absence makes the heart grow fonder

7. The mere-exposure effect provides one possible explanation for

   a. why proximity leads to liking
   b. why similarity leads to liking
   c. the equity phenomenon
   d. the matching phenomenon

8. In a study of arranged versus love-based marriages in India, researchers found that

   a. love-based marriages were more likely to survive
   b. those in arranged marriages experienced reactance and never felt feelings of love for their spouse
   c. after five years of marriage, those in love-based marriages reported diminished feelings of love while those in arranged marriages reported more love
   d. those in love-based marriages were more likely to demonstrate the disclosure reciprocity effect

9. Based on research presented in the text, if you go out on a blind date you would be most influenced by your date's

   a. open-mindedness
   b. sense of humor
   c. physical attractiveness
   d. sincerity

10. The finding that people pair off with others who are about as attractive as themselves is known as

   a. the matching phenomenon
   b. complementarity
   c. the reciprocity effect
   d. Gause's law

11. Which of the following seems to be true from research on social attraction?

   a. what is beautiful is judged to be good
   b. what is familiar is judged to be boring
   c. what is unique is judged to be valuable
   d. what is average is judged to be unattractive

12. The evolutionary perspective suggests that females are most attracted to males who show

   a. empathy, nurturance, and self-sacrifice
   b. similarity in beliefs, attitudes, and values
   c. an ability to provide and protect resources
   d. high self-esteem, extroversion, and self-efficacy

13. According to the text, differences in the psychological characteristics of attractive and unattractive people are

   a. innate
   b. in the eye of the beholder and really do not exist
   c. the result of self-fulfilling prophecies
   d. an example of how the researcher's values may determine the outcome of research

14. When shown a picture of an average young woman, men who had been watching three beautiful women on a television show rated her as _____ than did men who had not been watching the program.

   a. more attractive
   b. less attractive
   c. more intelligent
   d. less intelligent

15. Theodore Newcomb's study of unacquainted male transfer students who roomed together in a boarding house at the University of Michigan indicated that

   a. those whose attitudes and interests were initially most similar were most likely to form close friendships
   b. those whose attitudes and interests were initially complementary were most likely to form close friendships
   c. "similar" students formed friendships initially but, as the weeks passed, "complementary" students began to form friendships that turned out to be the most lasting
   d. friendships were initially formed within the boarding house but as time passed, these dissolved and were replaced by more lasting relationships with students living elsewhere

16. In terms of adult attachment styles, _____ individuals seem to be possessive and jealous while _____ individuals are less invested in relationships and more likely to leave them.

   a. secure; insecure
   b. anxious-ambivalent; avoidant
   c. avoidant; anxious-ambivalent
   d. insecure; apathetic

17. People who were asked to rank _____ reasons for going out with their boyfriend or girlfriend later expressed less love for their partner than did people who were asked to rank _____ reasons.

   a. companionate, romantic
   b. extrinsic, intrinsic
   c. intrinsic, extrinsic
   d. common, unique

18. Research on equity in interpersonal relationships suggests that

   a. a marriage contract is more likely to undermine than enhance the couple's love
   b. tit-for-tat exchanges decrease people's liking for one another in business relationships
   c. the principle is innate
   d. following the principle increases liking between males but decreases liking between females

19. French students' least favorite letter among the letters of the alphabet is

   a. the least frequent letter in the French language
   b. the hardest letter to draw
   c. the last letter of the alphabet
   d. the hardest letter to pronounce

20. Studies of the impact of the Internet on social relationships indicate that

    a. most people experience the Internet to be social isolating

    b. people show less liking for people whom they have conversed with online for twenty minutes that those met for the same time face-to face

    c. friendships and romantic relationships that form on the Internet are more likely to last for at least two years

    d. people perceive off-line relationships to be more important and close than Internet friendships

21. People seem to have a lower risk of divorce if they

    a. had parents who divorced

    b. live in a large town or city

    c. cohabited before marriage

    d. are religiously committed

22. The idea that we are attracted to people who are in some ways different from ourselves is an essential aspect of the

    a. companionate love hypothesis

    b. matching phenomenon

    c. complementarity hypothesis

    d. reward theory of attraction

23. Research suggests we may be most attracted to the person who

    a. has always said only positive things about us

    b. once said negative things about us but now evaluates us positively

    c. once said positive things but now evaluates us negatively

    d. generally says negative things about us but occasionally says something positive

24. Robert Sternberg views love as a triangle whose three sides include all of the following except

    a. friendship

    b. commitment

    c. intimacy

    d. passion

25. Compared to North Americans, Asians may be less vulnerable to disillusionment in love relationships because they

    a. are less susceptible to relative deprivation and to the adaptation-level phenomenon

    b. are more likely to substitute ludus for eros

    c. experience a greater variety of emotionally arousing situations that are steered into passionate love

    d. are less focused on personal feelings and more concerned with practical aspects of social attachments

26. According to two-factor theory, emotion is a result of

   a. motives and thoughts
   b. rewards and punishments
   c. nature and nurture
   d. arousal and a label

27. Compared to men who were interviewed on a low, solid bridge, men interviewed on a narrow, wobbly bridge liked a

   a. female interviewer more
   b. male interviewer more
   c. female interviewer less
   d. male interviewer less

28. Which of the following is true?

   a. Good health increases happiness more than bad health decreases it
   b. There are more words for positive emotions than for negative emotions
   c. Destructive acts harm close relationships more than constructive acts build them
   d. A good reputation is easier to acquire than a bad one

29. Studies of men and women falling in and out of love have revealed that men tend to

   a. fall more readily in love and more slowly out of love
   b. fall more readily in love and more readily out of love
   c. fall more slowly in love and more slowly out of love
   d. fall more slowly in love and more readily out of love

30. Which of the following is true of self-disclosure?

   a. disclosure begets disclosure
   b. a person who engages in self-disclosure is perceived as anxious
   c. a person who engages in self-disclosure is perceived as manipulative
   d. self-disclosure leads to infatuation but not to true love

31. Which of the following is true?

   a. companionate love typically leads to romantic love
   b. self-disclosure reduces feelings of romantic love
   c. companionate love is more likely to endure when both partners feel it to be equitable
   d. spouses who pray together are more likely to report conflict in their marriage

32. An employee who feels underpaid may demand an increase in wages or exert less effort at his or her task. This behavior is an

   a. attempt to restore equity
   b. attempt to achieve complementarity
   c. example of the matching phenomenon
   d. example of the overexposure effect

33. Tom, who tends to be extraverted, has just moved into the dormitory at Federal College. He is most likely to make friends with

    a. Bill, his next-door neighbor
    b. John, a chemistry major who lives across campus
    c. Michael, an introvert who lives on the next floor
    d. Stuart, a student who lives off campus and who loves dogs

34. Mary, who is attractive, very intelligent, and high in social status marries Tom who is also attractive, very intelligent, and high in social status. Their relationship is best understood as an example of

    a. the ingratiation effect
    b. complementarity
    c. the mere-exposure effect
    d. the matching phenomenon

35. Some years ago, a mysterious student enveloped in a big, black bag began attending a speech class at a state university. While the teacher knew the "Black Bag's" identity, the other students did not. As the semester progressed, the students' attitude toward the Black Bag changed from hostility to curiosity to friendship. What may best explain the students' change in attitude?

    a. exposure breeds liking
    b. stress produces affiliation
    c. boredom breeds a liking for the novel
    d. similarity attracts

36. Maria, a talkative, extraverted, young woman, is strongly attracted to Ronald, a quiet, introverted, middle-aged man. Mary's attraction to Ronald would be best explained by

    a. exchange theory
    b. the matching phenomenon
    c. the equity principle
    d. the complementarity hypothesis

37. You overhear a casual acquaintance express approval of you in the coffee shop. You are most likely to think well of that acquaintance if

    a. you had learned an hour earlier that you had received an average grade on a history test
    b. you had learned an hour earlier that you had failed a chemistry test
    c. the acquaintance is unattractive
    d. the acquaintance is engaged to be married

38. Phyllis tends to be possessive and jealous in relating to Mark, her boyfriend. She has repeatedly broken up with him and becomes very emotional when discussing conflicts with him. Phyllis's relationship with Mark demonstrates _____ attachment.

a. bipolar
b. insecure
c. avoidant
d. depressed

39. Bill and Sara's relationship becomes progressively more intimate as each engages in a bit more self-revelation in response to the other's self-disclosure. Their relationship is marked by the _____ effect.

a. disclosure reciprocity
b. mutual disinhibition
c. reciprocal disinhibition
d. reciprocal intimacy

40. A stranger rides the same bus you do to school every day. According to the "mere-exposure effect," as the days pass you will come to view the stranger

a. as merely another student
b. more unfavorably
c. more critically
d. more favorably

SHORT ESSAY QUESTIONS

Answer the following questions in the space provided.

1. List four powerful influences upon liking and friendship.

2. Why does proximity promote friendship?

3. What is the physical-attractiveness stereotype?

4. What is the complementarity hypothesis? What does research indicate regarding it?

5. Describe the reward theory of attraction.

6. How does the two-factor theory of emotion explain passionate love?

7. Compare and contrast passionate love with companionate love.

8. Explain the equity principle and discuss its relevance to friendship and love

9. Discuss the causes and effects of self-disclosure.

10. Identify four factors that are associated with a lower risk of divorce

ANSWER KEY

Chapter Review

1. belong

2. proximity
   interaction
   anticipation
   exposure

3. attractiveness
   matching
   stereotype
   good
   reproductive
   status

4. similarity
   complementarity
   opposites

5. like
   approval
   reverses

6. reward
   good

7. passion
   commitment

8. Passionate

9. label
   romantic

10. romantic
    follow
    men

11. Companionate
    intimate

12. attachments
    secure
    Anxious
    Avoidant

13. equity
    proportional
    formal
    friendship

14. self-disclosure
    most

15. 20
    educated
    religiously
    loyalty
    voice

Matching Terms

1. g
2. l
3. c
4. h
5. d
6. j

7. a
8. k
9. b
10. e
11. i
12. f

True-False Review

1.	T	14.	T
2.	T	15.	F
3.	F	16.	F
4.	F	17.	F
5.	T	18.	T
6.	T	19.	F
7.	T	20.	T
8.	F	21.	T
9.	F	22.	F
10.	F	23.	F
11.	T	24.	T
12.	T	25.	T
13.	T		

Multiple-Choice Practice Test

1.	a	21.	d
2.	d	22.	c
3.	a	23.	b
4.	b	24.	a
5.	d	25.	d
6.	a	26.	d
7.	a	27.	a
8.	c	28.	c
9.	c	29.	a
10.	a	30.	a
11.	a	31.	c
12.	c	32.	a
13.	c	33.	a
14.	b	34.	d
15.	a	35.	a
16.	b	36.	d
17.	b	37.	b
18.	a	38.	b
19.	a	39.	a
20.	c	40.	d

CHAPTER 12

ALTRUISM: HELPING OTHERS

After completing your study of this chapter you should be able to:

1. Define altruism.

2. Describe how social-exchange theory explains altruism.

3. Identify two social norms that may motivate altruism.

4. Describe how evolutionary psychology accounts for altruism.

5. Identify situational influences that enhance helpfulness.

6. Discuss personal influences that affect helping.

7. Identify who is likely to receive help.

8. Discuss how altruism can be increased.

CHAPTER REVIEW

Supply the words necessary to complete each of the following statements.

1. Altruism is a motive to increase another's _____ without conscious regard for one's _____.

WHY DO WE HELP?

2. Social-exchange theory states that helping, like other social behaviors, is guided by social _____ in which we aim to maximize our _____ and minimize our _____. Rewards for helping may be either _____ (for example, social approval) or _____

(for example, reducing one's own distress). Other psychologists believe that seeing someone in distress may lead us to feel _____ as well as distress and then our helping may be motivated by genuine _____.

3. Researchers have identified two social norms that seem to motivate altruism. The _____ norm is an expectation that people will help, not hurt, those who have helped them. The norm operates most effectively as people _____ respond to deeds earlier done to them. The social-_____ norm is an expectation that people will help those dependent upon them. We apply the norm selectively by giving aid to those who _____ it.

4. Evolutionary psychology contends that the essence of life is gene _____ and thus we are programmed to be selfish. However, two forms of altruism that are favored by natural selection are _____ protection and _____. Most evolutionary psychologists believe that, since people are born selfish, we must _____ altruism.

5. The three theories of altruism _____ one another in offering different levels of explanation. Yet each is vulnerable to charges of being speculative and of merely explaining-by-_____.

WHEN WILL WE HELP?

6. As the number of bystanders at an emergency increases, any given bystander is less likely to _____ the incident, less likely to _____ it as an emergency, and less likely to assume _____ for taking action. This is especially true when the situation is _____ and the other bystanders are _____ who cannot easily detect one another's alarm.

7. People are likely to help after seeing someone else _____ and when they are not in a _____.

8. People are _____ willing to help after transgressing, apparently in order to relieve private _____ and to restore a positive public image. People who are in a _____ mood also tend to be altruistic especially when being helpful is a way of altering their mood. This "feel bad-do good" effect is generally not found in _____. Finally, people who are in a _____ mood are consistently more helpful.

9. Early research found only _____ relationships between personality variables and helping. The _____ of the person and situation is clearly seen in research comparing the helpfulness of males and females.

_____ predicts long-term altruism as reflected in volunteerism and charitable contributions.

WHOM DO WE HELP?

10. We are most likely to help those who both need and _____ it and those who are _____ to us. In crisis situations, women receive _____ offers of help than men, especially from men.

HOW CAN WE INCREASE HELPING?

11. One way to promote altruism is to _____ those factors that inhibit altruism. According to the decision tree, assisting people to _____ an incident correctly, and to assume _____ for intervening, should increase their involvement. Research shows that _____ asking people for help and making them more _____-aware promotes altruism.

12. Reprimands and the door-in-the-_____ technique promote helping by evoking _____ feelings and concern for one's self-image.

13. We can also _____ altruism. For example, research indicates that television's prosocial _____ have even greater effects on children than its antisocial ones.

14. The _____ effect suggests that we not use excessive rewards or threats in socializing altruism. If people are provided with just enough justification to help, they will view themselves as _____ persons and be more helpful. Finally, students who have heard about _____ on altruism are more helpful.

MATCHING TERMS

Write the letter of the correct term from the right before the appropriate number on the left.

_____ 1. An expectation that people will help those dependent upon them.

_____ 2. The classic illustration of altruism.

_____ 3. A person is less likely to provide help when others are present.

_____ 4. Seeing another's suffering may produce this.

_____ 5. Altruism that promotes gene survival.

_____ 6. Concern for one's self-image makes this effective.

_____ 7. Noticing, interpreting, assuming responsibility.

_____ 8. May prevent people who have helped from feeling altruistic.

_____ 9. The motivation to increase one's own welfare.

_____ 10. An effective means of socializing altruism.

_____ 11. Overestimating others' ability to read our emotions.

_____ 12. An expectation that people will help, not hurt, those who have helped them.

_____ 13. Perceiving certain individuals as outside the boundary within which one applies rules of fairness.

a. door-in-the-face technique

b. overjustification effect

c. bystander effect

d. egoism

e. kin selection

f. moral exclusion

g. social-responsibility norm

h. reciprocity norm

i. decision tree

j. modeling

k. the Good Samaritan

l. empathy

m. illusion of transparency

Circle T if the statement is true and F if it is false.

T F 1. People will donate more money to a charity when offered a product such as candy or candles.

T F 2. According to social norms theory, we use a "minimax" strategy in relating to others.

T F 3. Psychologists are in agreement that all our behavior is ultimately aimed at our own welfare.

T F 4. Receiving unsolicited help can lower one's self-esteem.

T F 5. The social-responsibility norm is an expectation that people will help those who have helped them.

T F 6. Evolutionary psychology maintains that the essence of life is gene survival.

T F 7. Compared to people in nonurban areas, those in big cities are less willing to do small favors.

T F 8. Religious commitment is not correlated with long-term altruism.

T F 9. In contrast to the other theories of altruism, social norms theory is speculative and after-the-fact.

T F 10. As the number of bystanders increases, any given bystander is less likely to interpret an incident as an emergency.

T F 11. Choosing the form that assistance should take is one of the important steps in Latane and Darley's decision tree.

T F 12. Men more frequently help attractive women than those they see as unattractive.

T F 13. Female helpers are more likely to assist female victims than male victims.

T F 14. People consistently help those of the same race more readily than those of a different race.

T F 15. When we feel guilty we are more likely to help those around us.

T F 16. According to the text, the "feel bad-do good" phenomenon does not apply to the elderly.

T F 17. Self-focused grief promotes altruism.

T F 18. Happiness makes people self-focused and thus less willing to help.

T F 19. Compared to fraternal twins, genetically identical twins are noticeably more mutually supportive.

T F 20. When faced with potentially dangerous situations in which strangers need help, men are more likely to help than are women.

T F 21. Altruism increases when one expects later to meet and to talk with a victim and other witnesses.

T F 22. Research indicated that participants who had just completed a biographical questionnaire were more willing to help.

T F 23. The door-in-the-face technique is a strategy for increasing altruism.

T F 24. Research indicates that television's prosocial models actually have greater effects on viewers than its antisocial models have.

T F 25. One of the most effective ways of teaching altruism is through utilizing the overjustification effect.

MULTIPLE-CHOICE PRACTICE TEST

Circle the correct letter.

1. According to the text, the classic illustration of altruism is provided by

    a. the Kitty Genovese case
    b. the parable of the Good Samaritan
    c. the parable of the Prodigal Son
    d. President Lincoln's Emancipation Proclamation

2. "Social economics" is a term most closely associated with

    a. social norms theory   c. social-exchange theory
    b. evolutionary psychology   d. the decision tree

3. According to social-exchange theory we will help when

    a. the benefits are external and the costs are internal
    b. the benefits are greater than the costs
    c. the benefits and costs are proportional
    d. the benefits are smaller than the costs

4. According to Daniel Batson, genuine altruism may have its basis in feelings of

   a. happiness   c. guilt
   b. sadness   d. empathy

5. The misinterpretations of emotional states involved in the bystander effect are fed by

   a. an illusion of transparency
   b. an illusion of control
   c. illusory correlation
   d. the foot-in-the-door phenomenon

6. The social-responsibility norm is an expectation that people will

   a. help those dependent on them
   b. help those who have helped them
   c. assume responsibility for helping their parents
   d. assume responsibility for correcting past mistakes

7. According to sociologist Alvin Gouldner, a universal moral code is

   a. a norm of reciprocity   c. kin selection
   b. a norm of social responsibility   d. a norm of restitution

8. Altruism is to _____ as egoism is to _____.

   a. reciprocity norm; empathy
   b. self-esteem; need for achievement
   c. another's welfare; one's own welfare
   d. evolutionary psychology; social exchange theory

9. According to the text, one possible reason why people in big cities are less helpful is that

   a. they have not internalized the norm of social responsibility
   b. they are busier than those living in small towns
   c. they have a greater number of selfish genes
   d. reciprocity does not work as well in big cities as it does in small, isolated groups

10. A Gallup poll found that being "highly spiritually committed" was
    _____ with helping the poor and elderly.

   a. negatively correlated
   b. uncorrelated
   c. positively correlated
   d. positively correlated for women and negatively correlated for men

11. Since we are born selfish, evolutionary psychologists propose that we attempt to

   a. develop a drug that will encourage altruism
   b. develop an "altruistic gene"
   c. teach altruism
   d. live only in small, isolated communities

12. According to the text, which theory of altruism proposes two types of altruism: a tit-for-tat reciprocal exchange, and a more unconditional helpfulness?

   a. social norms theory
   b. evolutionary psychology
   c. social-exchange theory
   d. all of the above

13. Latane and Darley attempted to explain people's failure to intervene in cases like that of Kitty Genovese in terms of

   a. a situational influence
   b. a personality trait
   c. a mood factor
   d. selfish genes

14. Researchers had participants fill out a questionnaire in a room either by themselves or with two strangers. When the experimenters pumped smoke through a wall vent, solitary participants

   a. noticed the smoke more quickly than did those in groups
   b. were more likely to misinterpret the smoke as being truth gas
   c. were less likely to seek help
   d. finished the questionnaire more quickly

15. What is meant by the term "bystander effect"?

   a. people are likely to gather at the scene of a serious accident
   b. people are likely to gather at the scene of a fire and hinder rescue operations
   c. people are more likely to provide aid when there are helping models present
   d. people are less likely to provide help when there are other bystanders

16. Which of the following is not one of the steps in Darley and Latane's decision tree?

   a. noticing the incident
   b. interpreting the incident as an emergency
   c. weighing the costs and benefits of helping
   d. assuming responsibility for intervening

17. According to the text, the presence of others may not inhibit helping if the bystanders

    a. can read each other's reactions
    b. are all of the same sex
    c. have a high level of education
    d. are members of one of the helping professions

18. When participants in Darley and Latane's seizure experiment were later interviewed,

    a. most said they thought the deception used by the experimenter was justified but they would not be willing to take part in future similar experiments because of the stress
    b. most said they did not think the deception was justified but they would take part in future similar experiments
    c. most said they did not think the deception was justified and they would not take part in future similar experiments
    d. all said they thought the deception was justified and would be willing to take part in future similar experiments

19. According to the text, people in a hurry may be less willing to help because

    a. they have weighed the costs of helping and have decided they are too high
    b. they never fully grasp the situation as one requiring their assistance
    c. they tend to be selfish and primarily concerned with meeting their own needs
    d. they tend to be in a negative mood state and therefore are less likely to help

20. Researchers who have investigated the relationship between empathy and altruism

    a. agree that empathy leads to genuine altruism
    b. agree that empathy leads to helping that is egoistically motivated
    c. agree that empathy leads to pure altruism in females but not in males
    d. debate whether empathy leads to pure altruism

21. Which of the following negative moods is most likely to motivate altruism?

    a. depression   c. guilt
    b. anger   d. grief

22. Research suggests that we are especially likely to help when

    a. we are happy
    b. others are present and are doing nothing
    c. the potential recipient of our help is of the opposite sex
    d. the potential recipient of our help is of a different nationality

23. In comparison to low self-monitors, high self-monitors are especially helpful if

    a. they are led to think that helpfulness will be socially rewarded
    b. the social-responsibility norm is salient
    c. they are exposed to altruistic models
    d. they experience empathy

24. Batson found that those who attributed their helpful act to compliance rather than compassion

    a. subsequently volunteered less time to a service agency
    b. demonstrated reactance and ended up feeling more empathy for the person they helped
    c. felt guilty and responded more positively to a new request for help
    d. were subsequently more aware of the reciprocity norm

25. Rewards and costs are to _____ as gene survival is to _____.

    a. social-exchange theory; social norms theory
    b. sociobiology; social norms theory
    c. social norms theory; evolutionary psychology
    d. social-exchange theory; evolutionary psychology

26. Research has indicated that when students have been informed through a lecture of how bystanders can affect one's reactions to an emergency, the

    a. students are subsequently more likely to help someone in need
    b. students' willingness to help is unchanged for they refuse to believe they can be influenced by other people
    c. students' willingness to help is increased for a few hours following the lecture but for no longer
    d. students' willingness to help actually decreases due to psychological reactance

27. Research suggests that those who are high in _____ are more likely to be helpful.

    a. authoritarianism   c. extroversion
    b. self-efficacy   d. achievement motivation

28. Research indicates that compared to adults, young children are

    a. more likely to help
    b. less likely to help when they are busy
    c. less likely to help when they are sad
    d. less likely to help when they are watching television

29. What does research indicate regarding the role of gender difference in predicting helping?

    a. gender is unrelated to helping
    b. males are more helpful than females
    c. females are more helpful than males
    d. gender difference interacts with the situation

30. According to the text, the door-in-the-face technique works to promote altruism because people are

    a. provided a helpful model to imitate
    b. in a happy mood
    c. concerned about their self-image
    d. distracted from self-concern

31. When a solicitor for a charitable cause added the phrase, "Even a penny will help" to the request for a donation,

    a. the total number of contributors increased but the average amount of each contribution decreased
    b. both the number of contributors and the average amount of each contribution decreased
    c. both the number of contributors and the average amount of each contribution increased
    d. the total number of contributors decreased but the average amount of each contribution increased

32. In socializing altruism, we should beware of the

    a. overjustification effect   c. fundamental attribution error
    b. underjustification effect   d. foot-in-the-door effect

33. Which of the following religious teachings most clearly promotes "moral inclusion"?

    a. "Love your neighbor as yourself"
    b. "Everyone is a child of God and thus your brother or sister"
    c. "Honor your father and your mother"
    d. "An eye for an eye and a tooth for a tooth"

34. You trip over a fallen branch and sprain your ankle. According to research on the bystander effect, a stranger who sees your plight will be most likely to offer aid if there are _____ others present.

    a. no   c. four
    b. two   d. ten

35. The statement, "There is no duty more indispensable than that of returning a kindness," reflects the _____ norm.

    a. restitution
    b. reciprocity
    c. social-responsibility
    d. equity

36. Who of the following is least likely to help an injured pedestrian?

    a. Peter who has just found $10 in a grocery store
    b. Anita who is five minutes late for a committee meeting
    c. Carol who has just lost a dollar bill in a poker game
    d. Ralph who is five minutes early for work

37. Your roommate asks you to loan her $25 to buy her boyfriend a birthday present and you refuse. She then asks for three dollars to purchase a new notebook. You loan her the three dollars. Your roommate has successfully used the

    a. overjustification effect
    b. insufficient justification effect
    c. door-in-the-face technique
    d. foot-in-the-door technique

38. From an evolutionary perspective it would be most difficult to explain why

    a. John paid his son's hospital bill
    b. Phyllis helps her mother clean the house
    c. William helps his next-door neighbor paint his house
    d. Ruth risked her life to save a stranger from being murdered

39. Which of the following techniques should elementary schoolteachers use if they hope to promote enduring altruistic tendencies in students?

    a. show them films of heroes who risked their own welfare to help others
    b. offer a prize to the boy or girl who is most helpful to other students in a two-week period
    c. reprimand and punish any overt aggression
    d. instill a sense of partriotism

40. When his car overheated on a nearly deserted highway early one morning, elderly Mr. Hurley received help from the first passerby. One week later the same thing happened in the afternoon when traffic was heavy, and Mr. Hurley waited nearly two hours for help. This difference best illustrates

    a. the overjustification effect
    b. social facilitation
    c. the illusion of transparency
    d. the bystander effect

SHORT ESSAY QUESTIONS

Answer the following questions in the space provided.

1. Define altruism.

2. What criticism has been made of social-exchange theory?

3. List two social norms that may motivate altruism and briefly explain each.

4. What two kinds of altruism are predicted by evolutionary psychology? Give a specific example of each.

5. Describe the steps in the decision tree for helping.

6. What is the relationship between mood and willingness to help?

7. What is the relationship between personality and willingness to help?

8. Describe whom we are most likely to help.

9. How can altruism be taught?

ANSWER KEY

Chapter Review

1. welfare
   self-interests

2. economics
   rewards
   costs
   external
   internal
   empathy
   altruism

3. reciprocity
   publicly
   responsibility
   deserve

4. survival
   kin
   reciprocity
   teach

5. complement
   naming

6. notice
   interpret
   responsibility
   ambiguous
   strangers

7. helping
   hurry

8. more
   guilt
   negative
   children
   positive

9. modest
   interaction
   Religiosity

10. deserve
    similar
    more

11. reverse
    interpret
    responsibility
    personally
    self

12. face
    guilt

13. teach
    models

14. overjustification
    altruistic
    research

Matching Terms

1. g	7. i
2. k	8. b
3. c	9. d
4. l	10. j
5. e	11. m
6. a	12. h
	13. f

True-False Review

1. T	14. F
2. F	15. T
3. F	16. F
4. T	17. F
5. F	18. F
6. T	19. T
7. T	20. T
8. F	21. T
9. F	22. T
10. T	23. T
11. F	24. T
12. T	25. F
13. F	

Multiple-Choice Practice Test

1.	b	21.	c
2.	c	22.	a
3.	b	23.	a
4.	d	24.	a
5.	a	25.	d
6.	a	26.	a
7.	a	27.	b
8.	c	28.	c
9.	d	29.	d
10.	c	30.	c
11.	c	31.	c
12.	d	32.	a
13.	a	33.	b
14.	a	34.	a
15.	d	35.	b
16.	c	36.	b
17.	a	37.	c
18.	d	38.	d
19.	b	39.	a
20.	d	40.	d

CHAPTER 13

CONFLICT AND PEACEMAKING

CHAPTER OBJECTIVES

After completing your study of this chapter you should be able to:

1. Define conflict.

2. Explain how the pursuit of self-interest can produce a social dilemma.

3. Suggest specific ways of resolving social dilemmas.

4. Describe how competition produces conflict.

5. Describe the criterion most people use to define justice.

6. Identify specific misperceptions that fuel conflict.

7. List the conditions under which close contact reduces hostility between opposing parties

8. Describe how superordinate goals reduce conflict.

9. Explain how bargaining, mediation, and arbitration can be used to resolve differences between opposing parties.

10. Describe the GRIT model for reducing conflict.

CHAPTER REVIEW

Supply the words necessary to complete each of the following statements.

CONFLICT

1. Conflict is a _____ incompatibility of actions or goals.

2. Social dilemmas such as nuclear arms, overpopulation, and natural resource depletion are the result of various parties rationally pursuing their _____ to their collective _____. The _____ Dilemma and the Tragedy of the _____ games have been used to study how well-meaning people easily become trapped in mutually destructive behavior.

3. Research with the laboratory dilemmas suggests that cooperation can be promoted by regulation, by keeping social groups _____ so that people feel responsibility for one another, by allowing people to _____ and thereby reducing mistrust, by changing the payoffs to make cooperation more rewarding, and by appeals to _____ norms.

4. _____ for scarce resources can also breed conflict. In a series of famous experiments, Sherif divided boys into two groups and found that win-_____ competition triggered outright warfare.

5. Many people believe the criterion for justice is _____, in which the distribution of rewards is in _____ to individuals' contributions. When people feel exploited, they may accept and justify their inferior position, demand _____, or attempt to restore _____ by retaliating.

6. Conflicts often contain only a small core of truly incompatible goals but are surrounded by many _____ of the other's motives and goals. Opposing parties often have _____ perceptions: Each attributes the same virtues to themselves and the same vices to the other. Such images are often self-_____. International conflicts are also fed by the evil _____-good _____ illusion.

PEACEMAKING

7. Early studies of desegregation, for example, in public housing, indicated that racial contact _____ prejudice. More recent studies show that desegregation of schools has _____ effect upon racial attitudes. Contact that is prolonged, intimate, and structured to convey _____ status often reduces conflict.

8. In his boys' camp experiments, Sherif demonstrated how conflict between groups promotes _____ within groups. He introduced _____ goals to reconcile opposing groups. Similarly, replacing competitive learning situations with opportunities for _____ learning improved race relations in desegregated schools.

9. Generalizing from positive interracial experiences may be enhanced by initially _____ group diversity, then acknowledging it, then _____ it.

10. When conflicts are not intense or at an impasse, opposing parties may _____ directly, that is, seek agreement through direct negotiation. Sometimes a third-party _____ can help antagonists by replacing their win-_____ view of the conflict with a more cooperative win-_____ orientation. They can also reduce _____ and increase mutual understanding and trust. _____ is resolution of a conflict by a neutral third party who studies both sides and imposes a solution.

11. Sometimes tension is so high that genuine communication becomes impossible. In such cases, small _____ acts by one party may elicit reciprocal actions from the other. In Osgood's _____ model, one party to a conflict _____ its conciliatory intent, invites the adversary to _____, carries out several verifiable conciliatory _____, and maintains its _____ capability.

MATCHING TERMS

Write the letter of the correct term from the right before the appropriate number on the left.

_____ 1. Uses conciliation to reduce tension.

_____ 2. Sherif's solution to conflict in a boys' summer camp.

_____ 3. A laboratory demonstration of the tragedy of the commons.

_____ 4. A third party imposes a settlement.

_____ 5. On any given trial in this game, one is better off confessing.

_____ 6. The distribution of rewards in proportion to individuals' contributions.

_____ 7. Arab and Israeli views.

_____ 8. A cooperative learning technique used in schools.

_____ 9. Contact between opposing groups must be of this sort if it is to reduce conflict.

_____ 10. An effort to synthesize aspects of both individualism and collectivism.

_____ 11. The opposing parties seek agreement through direct negotiation.

_____ 12. Competition produced conflict and a common goal reduced it.

_____ 13. A third party facilitates communication between two opposing groups.

a. Edney's Nuts Game

b. equity

c. superordinate goal

d. mirror-image perceptions

e. Rattlers and Eagles

f. GRIT

g. jigsaw technique

h. equal status

i. mediation

j. arbitration

k. bargaining

l. Prisoner's Dilemma

m. communitarianism

Circle T if the statement is true and F if it is false.

T F 1. Conflict is always a destructive drain on human potential.

T F 2. Conflict is a perceived incompatibility of actions or goals.

T F 3. In the Prisoner's Dilemma, a person always receives the best payoff on a particular trial if he or she cooperates.

T F 4. The laboratory dilemmas provide examples of how well-meaning people become trapped into mutually destructive behavior.

T F 5. The "tragedy of the commons" refers to the loss of one's personal property when it is taken over by the government.

T F 6. Aronson's use of the "jigsaw" technique demonstrates how conciliation reduces conflict.

T F 7. The Prisoner's Dilemma is an example of a non-zero-sum game.

T F 8. In laboratory dilemmas people who realize that their self-serving choices are mutually destructive stop making them.

T F 9. Integrative agreements are win-win agreements that reconcile both parties' interests to their mutual benefit.

T F 10. Sherif's experiments in a boys' summer camp demonstrated how competition can produce social conflict.

T F 11. All cultures tend to define justice in terms of equity.

T F 12. Equity involves the distribution of rewards in proportion to individuals' needs.

T F 13. People with opposing views on issues such as abortion and capital punishment often differ less than they suppose.

T F 14. Conflicts often contain only a small number of truly incompatible goals.

T F 15. After reading about the commons dilemma, theater patrons littered less than those who had read about voting.

T F 16. Student exchange programs invariably improve students' attitudes toward their host countries.

T F 17. Results of school desegregation studies have shown that interracial contact consistently reduces prejudice.

T F 18. Sherif used arbitration to reduce conflict in the boys' summer camp.

T F 19. Cooperative learning strategies have been shown to improve race relations in desegregated schools.

T F 20. Mediation involves resolution of a conflict by a third party who studies both sides and imposes a settlement.

T F 21. The Kennedy experiment demonstrates how arbitration can reduce conflict.

T F 22. If you want to buy a new car at the best price, adopting a tough bargaining stance by opening with a very low offer generally backfires.

T F 23. GRIT uses conciliation to reduce conflict.

T F 24. Studies of American and Soviet political statements indicated that while Americans preferred mutual disarmament, the Soviets preferred to obtain military superiority.

T F 25. In laboratory games those who are 100 percent cooperative are rarely exploited.

MULTIPLE-CHOICE PRACTICE TEST

Circle the correct letter.

1. Which of the following is true of conflict?

   a. without conflict, people seldom face and resolve their problems
   b. conflict always involves a real incompatibility of goals
   c. social psychologists have studied interpersonal but not international conflict
   d. social psychologists have not been able to study conflict in a laboratory setting

2. The tragedy of the commons illustrates how

   a. communism leads to economic ruin
   b. self-serving behavior leads to collective doom
   c. false stereotypes lead to social conflict
   d. superordinate goals may fail to produce cooperation in capitalistic societies

3. Edney's Nuts Game

    a. is a non-zero-sum game played between two persons
    b. demonstrates how mirror-image perceptions can increase conflict
    c. demonstrates how conciliation reduces conflict
    d. illustrates the tragedy of the commons

4. In non-zero-sum games,

    a. one player always wins and the other always loses
    b. one player's winnings equal the other player's losses
    c. both players may win, both may lose, or one may win and the other may lose
    d. the players' combined outcomes can never equal zero

5. The _____ the commons, the _____ responsibility each person feels for it.

    a. smaller; more   c. more important; more
    b. larger; more   d. more important; less

6. Research on laboratory dilemmas reveals that cooperation is facilitated if

    a. one person is 100 percent cooperative
    b. the opponents can communicate with one another
    c. the game is changed into a zero-sum game
    d. the size of the payoffs is increased

7. Appeals to altruistic norms

    a. have proven to be helpful in reducing social dilemmas
    b. work in resolving small-scale but not large-scale dilemmas
    c. create reactance and make people more competitive
    d. work to resolve conflict in the Nuts Game but not in the Prisoner's Dilemma

8. Sherif's experiments in a boys' summer camp demonstrated how _____ reduce conflict.

    a. appeals to altruistic norms   c. communications
    b. regulations   d. superordinate goals

9. People are likely to have high self-esteem if they have a _____ ethnic identity and a _____ mainstream cultural identity.

   a. weak; weak
   b. weak; strong
   c. strong; weak
   d. strong; strong

10. In Japan, pay is more often based on _____ and less often based on _____.

    a. need; equality
    b. education; experience
    c. seniority; productivity
    d. potential; achievement

11. According to the text, the integration of major league baseball with the arrival of Jackie Robinson included all of the following <u>except</u>

    a. the offer of final-offer arbitration
    b. establishing equal status contact with a superordinate goal
    c. individuating the new group member
    d. creating a perception that change is inevitable

12. When Gregory Mitchell and his colleagues asked American University students what standard of justice they would prefer if their own place on the economic ladder was unknown, they indicated that they would prefer

    a. that resources be distributed equally
    b. that resources be distributed on the basis of productivity
    c. enough priority placed on equality to meet their own needs but also some reward for productivity
    d. that goods be distributed strictly on the basis of need

13. Shared goals that necessitate cooperative effort are said to be

    a. reciprocal
    b. superordinate
    c. equitable
    d. companionate

14. The tendency of each party to a conflict to see itself as moral and peaceloving and the other as evil and aggressive is known as

    a. reciprocal illusory perceptions
    b. the fundamental attribution error
    c. illusory correlation
    d. mirror-image perception

15. According to Walter Stephan's review of the research, what has been the influence of school desegregation on racial attitudes in the United States?

   a. overall, racial attitudes seem to have been little affected
   b. hostility has increased
   c. hostility has decreased
   d. hostility has increased in the South but decreased in the North

16. Contact between opposing racial groups reduces hostility

   a. if it occurs in a competitive situation where parties are likely to communicate with each other
   b. if the minority group is given superior status
   c. if it is structured to convey equal status
   d. between younger members of the respective groups but not between older members

17. Conflict between groups promotes _____ within groups.

   a. unity
   b. conflict
   c. concern for equity
   d. role confusion

18. Studies of the use of cooperative learning strategies in the schools have shown that such strategies can

   a. increase self-esteem
   b. increase liking for school
   c. improve race relations
   d. do all of the above

19. Which of the following is a cooperative learning strategy used in schools?

   a. the GRIT model
   b. the jigsaw technique
   c. the Nuts Game
   d. the Simulated Mediation Game

20. Bargaining tough is likely to backfire

   a. when the conflict is over a pie of fixed size
   b. when the conflict is over a pie that can shrink
   c. when females bargain tough with males
   d. in virtually every situation

21. The GRIT strategy was formulated as a plan

   a. for reversing conflict through conciliation
   b. for decreasing interracial tensions in desegregated schools
   c. to demonstrate how conflict in general can be reduced through arbitration
   d. to demonstrate how regulation can alleviate social dilemmas

22. In playing the laboratory version of Prisoner's Dilemma, a person's outcome from <u>any given decision</u> will be better if he or she

    a. cooperates
    b. defects
    c. cooperates only if the other person cooperates
    d. cooperates only if the other person defects

23. When Kaori Sato used a simulated forest to study the Commons Dilemma in a communal culture, he found

    a. results much like those obtained in western cultures
    b. that people were much more cooperative than in western cultures
    c. females but not males were more cooperative than their counterparts in western cultures
    d. adults but not children were more cooperative than their counterparts in western cultures

24. When Robyn Dawes and his colleagues gave people a short sermon about group benefits, exploitation, and ethics before they played a dilemma game,

    a. people reacted by playing even more competitively
    b. people were more cooperative in their play
    c. people ignored the sermon and their play was unchanged
    d. females were more cooperative and males were more competitive

25. A cooperative effort engaged in by two previously conflicting groups

    a. always has the long-term effect of boosting the groups' attraction to one another
    b. may actually increase tension between the two groups if the effort is unsuccessful
    c. will only be effective in reducing long-term tensions if engaging in the effort was suggested by a mediator
    d. typically reduces long-term conflict between opposing groups of males but not between opposing groups of females

26. Compared to compromises, integrative agreements are

    a. more enduring and lead to better ongoing relationships
    b. only reached through mediation or arbitration
    c. only possible when perceived injustice is the cause of conflict
    d. less likely to lead to a permanent settlement

27. We are most likely to generalize positive interracial experiences with a few individuals to a more positive attitude toward a whole outgroup if we perceive

   a. the outgroup as being as diverse as our own group
   b. the individuals as being representative of their group rather than as atypical
   c. ourselves as the only members from our own group having positive experiences with the outgroup
   d. the individuals as high in social status within the outgroup

28. In "final-offer arbitration," the third party settles a conflict by

   a. choosing between the final offers made by each side
   b. compromising between the final offers made by each side
   c. providing an integrative agreement based on final offers from each side
   d. introducing a superordinate goal

29. A key factor in determining whether people will communicate constructively and thereby correct misperceptions is

   a. their trust that the opposing side is well-intentioned
   b. their verbal fluency
   c. if each party sticks to statements of fact and refrains from stating how they feel about the other's actions
   d. if information which contradicts the other party's misperceptions is given bit by bit and not all at once

30. The "Kennedy experiment" was an application of _____ to international tension reduction.

   a. equal status contact   c. arbitration
   b. the jigsaw technique   d. the GRIT model

31. Two gas station owners in Roseville cut their gas prices in order to capture a portion of their competitor's business. However, neither gained any of the other's customers and in the long run both operated at a loss. This outcome best illustrates the dynamics of

   a. a social dilemma   c. an inequitable relationship
   b. the GRIT strategy   d. mirror-image perceptions

32. Rodney and Ralph are twin brothers who each contributed $75 to purchase a new bicycle. Rodney rides it 75 percent of the time. This would be an example of

   a. an inequitable relationship   c. a zero-sum relationship
   b. the tragedy of the commons   d. mirror-image perceptions

33. John believes he is hard-working but his wife Rachel is lazy. Rachel believes she is hard-working but John is lazy. This is an example of

    a. an inequitable relationship   c. a superordinate conflict
    b. mirror-image perception   d. a social trap

34. Which of the following best illustrates a superordinate goal?

    a. a college student who has been failing English gets an "A" on a paper
    b. a woman beats her husband at tennis
    c. apartment dwellers install a television antenna they can all use
    d. an obese person loses 20 pounds in two weeks

35. According to the text, contact between two conflicting racial groups can often improve relationships and correct misperceptions. Which kind of contact is, however, least likely to have that effect?

    a. placing Black and White athletes on the same baseball team
    b. having Black and White employees work together in small groups in an industrial plant
    c. placing White policemen on duty in predominantly Black residential neighborhoods
    d. having Blacks and Whites move into the same apartment building

36. Sherif's studies of conflict in summer camp should lead one to suggest which of the following to a couple having marital difficulties?

    a. play poker, keeping a cumulative score
    b. encounter each other: express your true feelings
    c. work together on something
    d. take separate vacations

37. Factory workers want a pay rate of $18 per hour and management offers $14 per hour. After weeks of conflict they agree to have a third party set the pay scale. After hearing both sides the third party sets the rate at $16. This is an example of resolving conflict through

    a. bargaining   c. mediation
    b. arbitration   d. conciliation

38. The GRIT model could be applied to the reduction of conflict between

    a. individuals   c. nations
    b. groups   d. all of these

39. Milton, a Jewish-American, lacks a real sense of either his Jewish or his American identity Milton is especially likely to experience

   a. mirror-image perceptions
   b. ingroup bias
   c. low self-esteem
   d. the tragedy of the commons

40. Kevin and Joel, two teenage brothers, are fighting over the evening newspaper. Knowing Kevin only wants the sports section and Joel only wants the latest stock quotations, their mother takes the paper and gives each boy the section containing the news of interest. In this case the mother arrived at a(n)

   a. mutual compromise
   b. cooperative settlement
   c. enlightened consensus
   d. integrative agreement

SHORT ESSAY QUESTIONS

Answer the following questions in the space provided.

1. Define conflict.

2. Describe the "tragedy of the commons" and explain its causes.

3. List three possible ways of promoting cooperation in the Prisoner's Dilemma game.

4. Briefly describe how Sherif first increased and then decreased conflict in a boys' summer camp.

5. Give the formula for an equitable relationship.

6. Under what conditions is desegregation likely to lead to improved race relations?

7. Distinguish between bargaining, mediation, and arbitration.

8. Describe the GRIT strategy for reducing conflict.

Chapter Review

1. perceived

2. self-interest
   detriment
   Prisoner's
   Commons

3. small
   communicate
   altruistic

4. Competition
   lose

5. equity
   proportion
   compensation
   equity

6. misperceptions
   mirror-image
   confirming
   leader
   people

7. reduces
   little
   equal

8. unity
   superordinate
   cooperative

9. minimizing
   transcending

10. bargain
    mediator
    lose
    win
    misperceptions
    Arbitration

11. conciliatory
    GRIT
    announces
    reciprocate
    actions
    retaliatory

Matching Terms

1. f
2. c
3. a
4. j
5. l
6. b

7. d
8. g
9. h
10. m
11. k
12. e
13. i

True-False Review

1.	F	14.	T
2.	T	15.	T
3.	F	16.	F
4.	T	17.	F
5.	F	18.	F
6.	F	19.	T
7.	T	20.	F
8.	F	21.	F
9.	T	22.	F
10.	T	23.	T
11.	F	24.	F
12.	F	25.	F
13.	T		

Multiple-Choice Practice Test

1.	a	21.	a
2.	b	22.	b
3.	d	23.	a
4.	c	24.	b
5.	a	25.	b
6.	b	26.	a
7.	a	27.	b
8.	d	28.	a
9.	d	29.	a
10.	c	30.	d
11.	a	31.	a
12.	c	32.	a
13.	b	33.	b
14.	d	34.	c
15.	a	35.	c
16.	c	36.	c
17.	a	37.	b
18.	d	38.	d
19.	b	39.	c
20.	b	40.	d

MODULE A

SOCIAL PSYCHOLOGY IN THE CLINIC

<u>CHAPTER OBJECTIVES</u>

After completing your study of this chapter you should be able to:

1. Describe how thinking errors may contaminate the personality interpretations made by mental health professionals.

2. Discuss implications of illusory thinking principles for psychology as a scientific discipline.

3. Describe the thought patterns of depressed persons and discuss whether their attributions are a cause or consequence of their depressed mood.

4. Describe the thought patterns associated with loneliness and social anxiety.

5. Discuss factors influencing people's reactions to illness and the role of negative emotions in health.

6. Identify social-psychological principles that can usefully be applied in treating psychological disorders.

7. Discuss the links between close relationships and well-being.

<u>CHAPTER REVIEW</u>

Supply the words necessary to complete each of the following statements.

1. Social psychology has contributed to improving the process of clinical
_____ and prediction, and to the understanding and _____ of
psychological _____.

MAKING CLINICAL JUDGMENTS

2. Professional clinical judgment is also social judgment, subject to its principles. _____ _____ is evident when clinicians perceive expected relationships between test performances and symptoms when no relationship exists. After-the-fact psychologizing is particularly vulnerable to the _____ bias.

3. When interacting with clients, erroneous diagnoses are often _____ since interviewers tend to seek out and recall information which _____ whatever they are looking for. The behaviors of people undergoing psychotherapy may come to fit the _____ of their therapists. Although statistical predictions may be unreliable, human _____ is even more unreliable.

4. The pervasiveness of _____ thinking points to a need for a _____ of human thought and behavior for it can help us sift truth from falsehood.

SOCIAL COGNITION IN PROBLEM BEHAVIORS

5. Although depressed people are _____ thinkers, research indicates that they make surprisingly _____ judgments. Depressed people are more likely to attribute failure to causes that are _____, global, and _____.

6. Our _____ color our thinking. Depression definitely has both cognitive and _____ consequences. At the same time, evidence suggests that a pessimistic _____ style contributes to depressive reactions.

7. Those who suffer chronic _____ and states of social _____ are also caught in a vicious cycle of self-defeating social _____ and social _____. _____ is a form of social anxiety characterized by self-consciousness and worry about what others think.

8. The new subfield of _____ psychology provides psychology's contribution to _____ medicine. It explores how people decide they are _____, how they explain their _____, and when they seek and follow _____. Heart disease has been linked with an _____-_____ personality. Research suggests that an attitude of _____ is good for health.

SOCIAL-PSYCHOLOGICAL APPROACHES TO TREATMENT

9. In treating psychological disorders some therapists assume that internal change can be triggered by changes in _____. Experiments indicate that the things

we say about ourselves can influence how we inwardly _____. This is particularly true when we feel _____ for how we have presented ourselves.

10. A self-defeating cycle of negative attitudes and behaviors can be broken by training more _____ behavior, by positive experiences that alter _____, and by directly modifying negative _____ patterns.

11. Improved states are most likely to be maintained if people attribute their improvement to _____ factors rather than to the _____ program itself.

12. Psychologists increasingly accept the idea that social _____ is at the heart of therapy. Therapists, aided by their image as _____ communicators, aim to stimulate healthier _____ by offering cogent arguments and raising questions. The _____ route to persuasion provides the most enduring attitude and behavior change.

SOCIAL SUPPORT AND WELL-BEING

13. Close, supportive relationships promote _____ and happiness. Such relationships assist people's coping with _____, especially when they enable people to _____ their intimate emotions.

14. Close relationships also foster _____. Throughout the world, _____ people report greater happiness and are less at risk for _____.

MATCHING TERMS

Write the letter of the correct term from the right before the appropriate number on the left.

_____ 1. About 10 percent of men and 20 percent of women will experience it.	a. clinical psychology
	b. loneliness
_____ 2. A distinguishing feature of depressed persons.	c. major depressive episode
_____ 3. Psychology's contribution to behavioral medicine.	d. explanatory style
_____ 4. May serve a self-handicapping function.	e. health psychology
	f. alcohol abuse
_____ 5. More common among adolescents than among adults.	g. behavioral medicine
_____ 6. Occurs when we are uncertain about our ability to impress others.	h. sadder-but-wiser
	i. self-confirming diagnosis
_____ 7. Integrates behavioral and medical knowledge about disease.	j. rational-emotive therapy
_____ 8. Teaches the depressed to accept credit for their successes.	k. explanatory style therapy
_____ 9. Patients come to fit the theories of their therapists.	l. social anxiety
_____ 10. Assumes emotions will follow behavior.	
_____ 11. One's habitual way of explaining life's events.	
_____ 12. The study, assessment, and treatment of people with psychological difficulties.	

TRUE-FALSE REVIEW

Circle T if the statement is true and F if it is false.

T F 1. Social psychology has contributed to the understanding but not to the treatment of psychological disorders.

T F 2. Mildly depressed people are more vulnerable to heart disease.

T F 3. In the hands of an experienced clinician, the Draw-a-Person test has very high predictive validity.

T F 4. Three out of four married people in the United States say their spouse is their best friend.

T F 5. Because of the ambiguity of their work, clinical psychologists tend to lack confidence in the accuracy of their judgments.

T F 6. In North America, young adults today are three times as likely as their grandparents to have suffered depression.

T F 7. After David Rosenhan alerted mental hospital staff members that pseudopatients might seek admission to their hospital, staff were much more accurate in recognizing real patients and those persons who were normal.

T F 8. In analyzing the childhood experiences of their clients, therapists can easily give after-the-fact interpretations that confirm their theories.

T F 9. The happiest university students are those who feel satisfied with their love life.

T F 10. The best predictor of success in graduate school is provided by the assessment of a trained interviewer.

T F 11. Close relationships promote psychological but not physical health.

T F 12. Research has indicated that depressed persons may be more accurate than nondepressives in estimating their degree of control over the environment.

T F 13. The most recent analyses of psychotherapeutic influence focus on how therapists establish credibility.

T F 14. Adolescents are more likely than adults to report feeling lonely.

T F 15. Males and females feel lonely under somewhat different conditions.

T F 16. Women's physical and mental skills fluctuate noticeably with their menstrual cycles.

T F 17. Alcohol abuse sometimes serves a self-handicapping function.

T F 18. Healthy behaviors are an essential contributor to the longevity of many optimists.

T F 19. Rates of suicide and depression are higher among the nonmarried.

T F 20. Explanatory style therapy attempts to alleviate depression by teaching victims to accept credit for their successes and to recognize how circumstances can make things go wrong.

T F 21. Intuitive or clinical predictions tend to be more reliable than statistical predictions.

T F 22. Depressed people are more likely than nondepressed people to blame themselves for their own failures.

T F 23. Depression is both a cause and a consequence of negative cognitions.

T F 24. Lonely people seem to have more negative perceptions of others.

T F 25. Increasingly psychologists believe that social influence is at the heart of psychotherapy.

MULTIPLE-CHOICE PRACTICE TEST

Circle the correct letter.

1. According to the text, social psychology has contributed to all of the following except

   a. our understanding of psychological disorders
   b. the treatment of psychological disorders
   c. improving the process of clinical judgment and prediction
   d. the definition of psychological disorder

2. The text suggests that clinicians may continue to have confidence in uninformative or ambiguous tests because of human susceptibility to

   a. the inoculation effect   c. the representativeness heuristic
   b. learned helplessness   d illusory correlation

3. After complaining of hearing voices, David Rosenhan and his associates were diagnosed as schizophrenic and hospitalized. Clinicians' subsequent attempts to explain the diagnosis demonstrated

   a. the bias in after-the-fact explanations
   b. the fundamental attribution error
   c. their susceptibility to the just world phenomenon
   d. the benefits of clinical intuition

4. Research on the relationship between marriage and happiness indicates that

   a. married men but not married women are happier than their single counterparts
   b. people who say their marriage is satisfying rarely report being unhappy or depressed
   c. about one-third of married Americans say their marriage is "very happy"
   d. happiness seems to promote marriage but marriage does not promote happiness

5. When people are asked, "What is necessary for your happiness?" most mention _____ first.

   a. meaningful work   c. close personal relationships
   b. money   d. good physical and mental health

6. From the material presented in the text, which of the following is an accurate statement?

   a. clinical psychologists are more susceptible to illusory thinking than are social psychologists
   b. projective tests actually give more useful information than do objective tests
   c. people who come for therapy want to hear negative things about themselves
   d. behaviors of people undergoing psychotherapy come to fit the theories of their therapists

7. Research evidence suggests that professional clinicians

   a. are relatively immune to the illusion of control
   b. should rely more heavily on clinical intuition than on statistical prediction
   c. are too readily convinced of their own after-the-fact analyses
   d. are more susceptible to illusory thinking than are social psychologists

8. Compared with college women who have experienced nonsexual traumas, sexually abused women reported more health problems especially if

   a. they had kept their secret to themselves
   b. the abuser was a relative
   c. they were high in self-monitoring
   d. they were planning to marry in the next year

9. According to the text, the pervasiveness of illusory thinking points to the need for a _____ study of thought and behavior.

   a. psychohistorical   c. scientific
   b. literary   d. humanistic

10. Which of the following attributions regarding a failure or setback illustrates the <u>stable</u> quality of a depressed person's explanatory style?

    a. "It's all my fault."
    b. "It's going to last forever."
    c. "The whole world is against me."
    d. "It's going to affect everything I do."

11. Studies of depression challenge the common presumption that

    a. depressed people are negative thinkers
    b. more women than men suffer major depressive episodes
    c. depressed people are unrealistic
    d. a depressed mood has both cognitive and behavioral consequences

12. Research on loneliness indicates that

    a. adults are more likely than adolescents to report feeling lonely
    b. lonely people are more realistic than those who do not report feelings of loneliness
    c. loneliness coincides with aloneness
    d. lonely people tend to perceive others in negative ways

13. When researchers had relatively depressed and nondepressed college students observe whether their pressing a button was linked with whether a light came on, the results indicated that the

    a. depressed underestimated their degree of control
    b. depressed were quite accurate in estimating their degree of control
    c. nondepressed were quite accurate in estimating their degree of control
    d. nondepressed underestimated their degree of control

14. Among U.S. residents, women _____ than men.

    a. have higher rates of cancer
    b. use fewer prescription drugs
    c. visit physicians more frequently
    d. report fewer symptoms of illness

15. Research on the social thinking of those vulnerable to depression indicates that

   a. depression is both a cause and a consequence of their negative thinking
   b. they have surprisingly positive self-concepts
   c. males and females who are depressed think very differently
   d. they are more vulnerable to both illusory correlation and the fundamental attribution error

16. Compared to nondepressed people, depressed people are more likely to attribute their failures and setbacks to causes that are

   a. unstable   c. internal
   b. specific   d. situational

17. According to Martin Seligman, the decline of religion and family and the growth of the "you can do it" idea have contributed to a large increase in

   a. character disorders   c. phobias
   b. schizophrenia   d. depression

18. Research indicates that heart disease is most clearly linked with an _____ personality.

   a. introverted   c. anger-prone
   b. apathetic   d. assertive

19. Members of baseball's Hall of Fame who offered pessimistic explanations for bad events such as losing big games

   a. died at younger ages
   b. were more susceptible to loneliness
   c. were less successful in life after retiring from baseball
   d. were more likely to be divorced

20. Satisfaction with _____ seems to be the best predictor of overall happiness.

   a work   c. finances
   b. marriage   d. community

21. Research suggests that an attitude of _____ is generally good for health.

   a. competitiveness   c. skepticism
   b. optimism   d. humility

22. In contrast to those who are not lonely, lonely people tend to

    a. spend more time talking about themselves when conversing with a stranger
    b. be more inclined to blame others for their problems
    c. be more susceptible to the illusion of control
    d. be more inclined to idealize members of the opposite sex

23. Brodt and Zimbardo found that shy women were no longer shy when they

    a. were provided an alternative explanation for their social anxiety
    b. were provided alcohol before interacting with others
    c. discovered most people feel shy
    d. were taught to blame their failures on circumstances beyond their control

24. Students who had been induced to write self-laudatory essays

    a. expressed higher self-esteem in private self-ratings
    b. were more likely to make the fundamental attribution error
    c. showed greater hostility to a stranger
    d. were more likely to rationalize their failure to help a person in need

25. Which of the following is not given as an example of a therapy that utilizes the "attitudes-follow-behavior" principle?

    a. assertiveness training   c. self-help groups
    b. rational-emotive therapy   d. psychoanalysis

26. Research suggests that optimists

    a. recover more slowly from coronary bypass surgery
    b. tend to offer stable, global, and internal explanations for bad events
    c. may see themselves as invulnerable and thus fail to take sensible precautions
    d. are less susceptible to depression but more susceptible to anxiety

27. Explanatory style therapy attempts to teach depressed people to

    a. accept credit for their successes and to note how circumstances make things go wrong
    b. avoid the fundamental attribution error
    c. attribute their depression to their own personality traits
    d. focus on others rather than on themselves

28. Graduates of a weight-control program were more successful in maintaining their weight loss if they had been

    a. led to credit their changed eating behavior to their own effort
    b. punished for violating rules of the treatment program
    c. promised large rewards for successfully losing weight
    d. led to credit their changed eating behavior to the therapist

29. Robyn Dawes, writing In House of Cards: Psychology and Psychotherapy Built on Myth, reports that interviewers' ratings of medical school applicants were highly predictive of the applicants'

    a. likelihood of receiving the M.D.
    b. eventual performance in their first year of residency
    c. likelihood of graduating from medical school with honors
    d. none of the above

30. Rats injected with live cancer cells were more likely to die of tumors if they also received _____.

    a. escapable shock   c. a high-fat diet
    b. inescapable shock   d. moderate doses of radiation

31. What error in thinking may contribute to a person's feeling of guilt after a close relative commits suicide?

    a. self-serving bias   c. the fundamental attribution error
    b. hindsight bias   d. depressive realism

32. The epidemic that suddenly affected Santa Monica students during a musical performance best illustrated the impact of

    a. perceived control on reactions to stress
    b. conditioning on the suppression of the immune system
    c. social influence on the interpretation of symptoms
    d. pessimism on physical health

33. Studies on people's reactions to their own physical condition indicate that

    a. half or more of all heart attack victims die before seeking or receiving medical help
    b. college students tend to overreport medical complaints
    c. women's mental skills fluctuate noticeably with their menstrual cycle
    d. most people are good at estimating their blood pressure

34. Chronically lonely people tend to blame _____ for their poor social relationships.

    a. their parents or early childhood experiences
    b. themselves
    c. the uncaring attitudes of the people around them
    d. cultural values and patterns

35. Dr. Jones is a psychologist who specializes in the causes and control of stress. Dr. Jones is most likely a(n) _____ psychologist.

    a. consumer
    b. educational
    c. forensic
    d. health

36. Philip suffers from chronic depression. How is he likely to respond when told that he failed the test to renew his driver's license?

    a. "Yesterday was just my unlucky day."
    b. "I imagine very few people have passed that same test."
    c. "The person giving the test is incompetent."
    d. "I am a poor driver and always will be."

37. Mary wants advice on how to cope with the stress of a new job. She would be best advised to approach her new job with a sense of

    a. skepticism and humility
    b. ambition and competitiveness
    c. urgency and time-consciousness
    d. control and optimism

38. As a result of participating in a program to help him quit smoking, Bill has not had a cigarette for three weeks. He is least likely to return to smoking if he attributes his success in quitting the habit to

    a. his own motivation
    b. the therapist who helped him quit
    c. the support of his friends
    d. the unique nature of the therapeutic program

39. Valerie is a mildly depressed college student. From research presented in the text on depression she

    a. probably suffers from the better-than-average phenomenon
    b. assumes that her behavior is well-accepted by others
    c. demonstrates the sadder-but-wiser effect
    d. is below average in intelligence

240

40. Gayle, a Freudian analyst, finds that, without exception, her patients report dreams closely related to their emotional problems and are easily understood in terms of Freud's theory of personality. From research presented in the text, what may best explain why the dreams and problems of Gayle's patients are so consistent with Freudian theory?

a. Freud's theory is the oldest and most comprehensive of all the theories of personality
b. Freud's theory is more ambiguous than any other theory, and thus any problem fits into its framework
c. the patients are perhaps induced to give information that is consistent with Gayle's theoretical orientation
d. Freudian psychotherapists are "true believers" and Gayle's report is an attempt to convert other therapists to her orientation

SHORT ESSAY QUESTIONS

Answer the following questions in the space provided.

1. Explain how each of the following may characterize the judgments of mental health professionals:

A. Illusory correlation

B. Hindsight bias

C. Self-fulfilling prophecy

2. Describe the thought patterns of depressed people. Is their attributional style the cause or the consequence of their depressed mood?

3. Describe the thought patterns associated with loneliness and social anxiety.

4. Describe how our emotions may influence our health.

5. Identify three social-psychological principles that may usefully be applied in the treatment of psychological disorders.

6. Briefly describe how social relations may influence health and happiness.

ANSWER KEY

Chapter Review

1. judgment
   treatment
   disorders

2. Illusory
   correlation
   hindsight

3. self-confirming
   verifies
   theories
   intuition

4. illusory
   science

5. negative
   accurate
   stable
   internal

6. moods
   behavioral
   explanatory

7. loneliness
   anxiety
   cognitions
   behaviors
   Shyness

8. health
   behavioral
   ill
   symptoms
   treatment
   anger-prone
   optimism

9. behavior
   feel
   responsible

10. skillful
    self-perceptions
    thought

11. internal
    treatment

12. influence
    credible
    thinking
    central

13. health
    stress
    confide

14. happiness
    married
    depression

Matching Terms

1. c
2. h
3. e
4. f
5. b
6. l

7. g
8. k
9. i
10. j
11. d
12. a

True-False Review

1. F	14. T
2. T	15. T
3. F	16. F
4. T	17. T
5. F	18. T
6. T	19. T
7. F	20. T
8. T	21. F
9. T	22. T
10. F	23. T
11. F	24. T
12. T	25. T
13. F	

Multiple-Choice Practice Test

1. d	21. b
2. d	22. a
3. a	23. a
4. b	24. a
5. c	25. d
6. d	26. c
7. c	27. a
8. a	28. a
9. c	29. d
10. b	30. b
11. c	31. b
12. d	32. c
13. b	33. a
14. c	34. b
15. a	35. d
16. c	36. d
17. d	37. d
18. c	38. a
19. a	39. c
20. b	40. c

MODULE B

SOCIAL PSYCHOLOGY IN COURT

CHAPTER OBJECTIVES

After completing your study of this chapter you should be able to:

1. Identify issues pertinent to both social psychology and the law.

2. Discuss findings on eyewitness testimony and describe ways of reducing error.

3. Identify defendant characteristics that may influence jurors' judgments and describe the effects of the judge's instructions.

4. Show how jurors' individual dispositions may influence their verdicts.

5. Discuss how a jury functions as a group.

6. Explain the value of simulated juries.

CHAPTER REVIEW

Supply the words necessary to complete each of the following statements.

1. We can think of the courtroom as a miniature social world; here, as elsewhere, people think about and _____ one another.

EYEWITNESS TESTIMONY

2. Experiments suggest that jurors find eyewitnesses _____, sometimes even those whose testimony is _____. In general, eyewitnesses' certainty about their judgments relates only modestly to their _____.

3. Errors creep in because we construct our _____ based partly on what we perceived at the time and partly on our expectations and beliefs. _____ what happened commits people to their recollections, whether

247

accurate or not. In addition, people tend to adjust what they say to _____

their listeners and then come to _____ their altered message.

Receiving confirming _____ increases eyewitnesses' confidence in their

judgments.

4. To increase the accuracy of eyewitnesses and jurors, experts suggest that we

_____ police interviewers, minimize _____ lineup

identifications, and educate jurors about _____ testimony.

OTHER INFLUENCES ON JUDGMENTS

5. The evidence usually is clear enough that jurors can set aside their

_____. But when the evidence is ambiguous, jurors may feel

sympathetic to a defendant who is _____ or who is

_____ to themselves. When jurors focus attention on the

_____, their biases seem to have minimal effect.

6. Jurors have difficulty following the judge's instructions to ignore _____

publicity or _____ evidence. One experiment found that a judge's

order to ignore testimony _____ to the testimony's impact.

7. _____ people about the inadmissibility of various types of

evidence diminishes its impact. _____ witnesses' testimony and

removing objectionable material provides another way of eliminating inadmissible

testimony.

THE JURORS AS INDIVIDUALS

8. In making decisions, jurors construct a story that makes sense of all the

_____, consider the judge's _____, and compare their

understanding with the possible _____. Despite the concern about

scientific jury _____, research indicates that _____ is

a more potent determinant of jurors' verdicts than their personal characteristics.

9. In a _____ case, the jurors' own characteristics can influence their

verdicts. For example, jurors who favor the _____ penalty appear more

likely to vote to convict certain types of defendants. They also tend to be more

_____, that is, rigid, punitive, and contemptuous of those with

lower social status.

THE JURY AS A GROUP

10. The chances are about two in _____ that jurors will initially not

agree on a verdict. Yet after discussion, _____ percent emerge with a

consensus.

11. The jury's verdict is usually the alternative favored by at least _____ of the jurors at the outset. Without such a majority, a _____ jury is likely to result.

12. Jurors in the minority are likely to be most persuasive when they are_____, persistent, and self-confident, especially if they begin to trigger _____ from the majority. Jurors who are _____ and of _____ social status tend to be most influential.

13. The finding that group deliberation leads high authoritarians to recommend _____ punishment and low authoritarians to recommend more _____ punishment suggests that group _____ can occur in juries.

14. When evidence is not highly incriminating, juries tend to become _____ lenient after deliberating. A minority that favors acquittal has a _____ chance than one that favors conviction. To the extent that _____ influence moves jurors, we can hope that a jury's collective judgment will be superior to that of its average member.

15. Recent research raises questions about the wisdom of several Supreme Court decisions permitting _____ juries and juries not required to reach _____. For example, juries not required to reach consensus seem to discuss _____ views rather superficially.

MATCHING TERMS

Write the letter of the correct term from the right before the appropriate number on the left.

_____ 1. Low authoritarians become more lenient, high authoritarians become more punitive.

_____ 2. Provides a way of eliminating inadmissible evidence.

_____ 3. Help researchers to formulate theories that can be used to interpret the complex world.

_____ 4. Persuasive but not always accurate.

_____ 5. May elicit reactance.

_____ 6. May discuss minority views rather superficially.

_____ 7. More concerned with crime control than with due process of law.

_____ 8. Without it a hung jury is likely.

_____ 9. Benefits the defendant.

_____ 10. Jurors' personal biases are more likely to influence the verdict.

_____ 11. Favoring acquittal, it stands a better chance.

_____ 12. Remembering wrong information.

a. misinformation effect

b. physical attractiveness

c. death-qualified jurors

d. judges' instructions

e. ambiguous cases

f. simulated juries

g. two-thirds majority

h. minority influence

i. group polarization

j. nonunanimous juries

k. videotaping

l. eyewitness testimony

TRUE-FALSE REVIEW

Circle T if the statement is true and F if it is false.

T F 1. According to the text, social psychologists have conducted experiments on the courtroom because it provides an excellent context for studying the effect of the physical environment on behavior.

T F 2. The U.S. Supreme Court has declared that one factor to be considered in judging eyewitness accuracy is the level of certainty demonstrated by the witness.

T F 3. Eyewitnesses who are shown to have poor eyesight may still have an impact on jurors judgments.

T F 4. Eyewitnesses' certainty about their own accuracy in viewing a crime is closely related to their actual accuracy.

T F 5. After suggestive questioning, witnesses may believe that a red light was actually green.

T F 6. The more we retell a story, the more we may convince ourselves of a falsehood.

T F 7. To increase eyewitness accuracy, interviewers should begin by allowing eyewitnesses to offer their own unprompted recollections.

T F 8. Live and videotaped testimony have much the same impact on jurors.

T F 9. Attractive defendants are treated more severely than unattractive defendants.

T F 10. Most jurors, when asked by a judge to "raise your hand if you've read anything about this case that would prejudice you," acknowledge their preconceptions.

T F 11. A person accused of a politically motivated burglary is judged less guilty if his political views are similar to those of the jurors.

T F 12. Simulated juries cannot provide helpful insights into the dynamics of actual courtrooms.

T F 13. When the evidence is clear and jurors focus on it, their biases seem to have minimal effect on their judgments.

T F 14. The U.S. Supreme Court has ruled that "death-qualified" jurors constitute a biased sample.

T F 15. False lineup identifications are reduced when witnesses simply make yes/no judgments in response to a sequence of people.

T F 16. The U.S. Supreme Court has disallowed five-member juries.

T F 17. When the evidence is not highly incriminating, jurors tend to become more lenient after deliberating.

T F 18. Hung juries occur in about 20 percent of all jury trials.

T F 19. People who favor the death penalty are also more prone to vote a defendant guilty.

T F 20. Research indicates that U.S. federal judges have sentenced Blacks to longer prison terms than Whites.

T F 21. One study of criminal and civil cases found that four times in five the judge concurred with the jury's decision.

T F 22. Smaller juries may be less likely to embody a community's diversity.

T F 23. Research indicates that 12-person juries are twice as likely as 6-person juries to have hung verdicts.

T F 24. Juries are more persuaded by evidence when it is presented in the order of a narrative story.

T F 25. Homicide rates have risen when states have abandoned the death penalty.

MULTIPLE-CHOICE PRACTICE TEST

Circle the correct letter.

1. From the text, which of the following is a <u>true</u> statement regarding social psychology and the courtroom?

   a. most of the government research funds available to social psychologists have been designated for the study of courtroom procedures
   b. the courtroom is a miniature social world where people think about and influence each other
   c. the study of criminal cases can provide important new insight into the causes of aggression and conflict
   d. social psychology had its roots in the study of the courtroom

252

2. Jurors who were asked to observe and evaluate eyewitnesses to the staged theft of a University of Alberta calculator

    a. believed both correct and incorrect eyewitnesses most of the time
    b. were suspicious of both correct and incorrect eyewitnesses
    c. believed the correct eyewitnesses but were suspicious of the incorrect eyewitnesses
    d. were suspicious of incorrect female eyewitnesses but tended to believe incorrect male eyewitnesses

3. Research suggests that eyewitnesses who correctly remember trivial details surrounding a crime

    a. also have a better memory for the culprit's face
    b. have a poorer memory for the culprit's face
    c. are less susceptible to misleading questions
    d. are more susceptible to misleading questions

4. Studies of the impact of eyewitness testimony indicate that

    a. eyewitnesses who have been discredited have no influence on a jury's judgments
    b. when witnessing conditions are shown to have been poor, jurors usually do not believe the eyewitness testimony
    c. eyewitnesses who are shown to have poor eyesight have no effect on the jurors' judgments
    d. none of the above are true

5. Research has indicated that false lineup identifications can be reduced by

    a. having witnesses make individual yes/no judgments in response to a sequence of people
    b. reminding witnesses that the offender may not be in the lineup
    c. using a "blank" lineup that contains no suspects and screening out those who make false identifications
    d. all of the above

6. Which of the following is not part of the literature discussed in the text on social psychology and the courtroom?

    a. how the defendant's characteristics can influence jurors' judgments
    b. how the jurors' own characteristics can influence their judgments
    c. how the physical environment of the jury room influences jurors' judgments
    d. how the judge's instructions influence jurors' judgments

7. Eyewitnesses who received confirming feedback on their testimony

   a. often felt manipulated and were less confident about their judgment
   b. recalled being more confident when making their initial judgment
   c. reported that the feedback significantly increased their confidence from when they made their initial judgment
   d. expressed greater liking for the experimenter and willingness to participate in additional research

8. When students were presented with a hypothetical robbery-murder with circumstantial evidence but no eyewitness testimony, only 18 percent voted for conviction. With the addition of eyewitness testimony to the circumstantial evidence,

   a. the majority of students voted for conviction provided the eyesight of the eyewitness was not called into question
   b. the majority of students voted for conviction even if the eyesight of the eyewitness was called into question
   c. 35 percent of the students voted for conviction provided the vision of the eyewitness was not called into question
   d. even fewer students voted for conviction if the eyesight of the witness was shown to be very poor

9. Students at California State University, Hayward, witnessed an assault on a professor. Seven weeks later when asked to identify the assailant from a group of six photographs,

   a. the majority made a wrong identification
   b. the majority chose the right person but distorted important details of the assault
   c. the majority of females chose the right person but the majority of males identified the wrong person
   d. upperclassmen were more accurate than freshmen in identifying the assailant

10. Research on memory construction indicates that suggestive questioning can lead people to believe that

    a. a yield sign was actually a stop sign
    b. a red light was actually green
    c. a robber had a moustache when he did not
    d. all of the above

11. Research indicates that having eyewitnesses rehearse their answers to questions before taking the witness stand

    a. raises uncertainty in the minds of eyewitnesses as to what they actually saw
    b. increases their confidence about what they saw
    c. increases their confidence but also heightens their anxiety about appearing in court
    d. invariably leads them to give a much more detailed and accurate account of what they saw

12. When experts provide jurors information on the conditions under which eyewitness accounts are trustworthy

    a. jurors become more likely to trust such testimony
    b. jurors demonstrate reactance and are even more likely to accept inaccurate testimony
    c. jurors are not influenced by the information experts provide
    d. less intelligent jurors demonstrate reactance but more intelligent jurors analyze eyewitness testimony more carefully

13. Research comparing juries' decisions with those made by a judge has indicated that

    a. when a judge disagrees with the jury's decision it is usually because the jury convicts someone the judge would acquit
    b. juries generally recommend longer prison terms than judges are inclined to give
    c. two-thirds of the time the jury and the judge disagree
    d. four times in five the judge concurs with the jury's decision

14. Research on the physical attractiveness of defendants has indicated that physically attractive defendants are

    a. less likely to be found guilty and if found guilty receive less punishment
    b. less likely to be found guilty but if found guilty receive more punishment
    c. more likely to be found guilty and if found guilty receive more punishment
    d. more likely to be found guilty but if found guilty receive less punishment

15. According to the text, a jury may demonstrate reactance in response to a

    a. dogmatic prosecuting attorney
    b. judge's instructions to ignore testimony
    c. self-confident eyewitness
    d. timid defense attorney

16. Videotaped testimony

    a.   allows the court to edit out inadmissible evidence
    b.   has been disallowed by the U.S. Supreme Court in real trials
    c.   does not have the same impact as live testimony
    d.   all of the above are true

17. In a study designed to test people's understanding of judicial instructions, viewers of videotaped instructions could answer _____ percent of the questions posed to them about what they had heard.

    a.   15   c.   65
    b.   40   d.   90

18. A judge's instructions to jurors that they ignore inadmissible evidence are most likely to be followed if given

    a.   immediately after the inadmissible evidence has been presented
    b.   as a forewarning before the evidence is presented
    c.   just before the jury retires to deliberate on the evidence
    d.   after the prosecution has presented its case but before the defense calls its witnesses

19. Survey researchers sometimes assist defense attorneys by using "scientific jury selection" to eliminate potential jurors likely to be unsympathetic. Results indicated that in the first nine important trials where the defense relied on such methods, it

    a.   won all nine
    b.   won two
    c.   won seven
    d.   lost all nine

20. In 1986, the U.S. Supreme Court in a split decision

    a.   ruled that death-qualified jurors are a biased sample
    b.   overturned a lower court ruling that death-qualified jurors are a biased sample
    c.   ruled that Georgia's five-member juries were as reliable and accurate as twelve-member juries
    d.   overturned a lower court decision that six-member juries could decide cases involving the death penalty

21. People who do not oppose the death penalty are

    a.   likely to have been involved in some crime themselves
    b.   more likely to favor the prosecution
    c.   likely to have deep religious convictions
    d.   likely to be middle-aged or elderly

22. Jurors who are more prone to vote guilty tend to be

    a. more authoritarian
    b. lower in self-esteem
    c. from the upper socioeconomic class
    d. higher in self-efficacy

23. Research on the individual characteristics of jurors, such as personality and general attitudes, indicates that

    a. these characteristics are as important as the evidence itself in determining jurors' verdicts
    b. these characteristics have their strongest effect when the evidence is ambiguous
    c. males are less likely to find a defendant guilty than are females
    d. highly religious persons are less likely to find a defendant guilty than are less religious persons

24. Someone accused of a crime is judged more sympathetically

    a. by females than by males
    b. if he or she appears to have personality characteristics that are complementary to the one who judges
    c. if he or she appears similar to the one who judges
    d. if there was a bystander who watched and did not intervene

25. Which of the following is true regarding the influence of minorities in jury deliberations?

    a. minorities composed of women are more influential than minorities composed of men
    b. frequently a minority view prevails and causes the majority to reverse its verdict
    c. a minority that favors acquittal stands a better chance of influencing the majority than does a minority that favors conviction
    d. minorities composed of high authoritarians are more influential than minorities composed of low authoritarians

26. What is meant by the "two-thirds-majority" scheme?

    a. two-thirds of all people asked refuse to serve on a jury
    b. two out of three times judges agree with the jury's decision
    c. a two-thirds majority is a better rule than consensus for a jury to follow in reaching a verdict
    d. the jury verdict is usually the alternative favored by at least two-thirds of the jurors at the outset

27. The fact that high authoritarians who initially recommended strong punishments were even more punitive after group deliberation suggests that _____ can occur in juries.

    a. group polarization   c. groupthink
    b. social facilitation   d. reactance

28. Jurors who are male and of high social status

    a. are overrepresented on juries
    b. tend to be most influential in simulated juries
    c. tend to produce reactance in female jurors
    d. are most likely to disregard a judge's instructions

29. From research on minority influence we can speculate that jurors in the minority

    a. will never have a significant effect on the majority
    b. may be persuasive if they state their case tentatively
    c. may be persuasive if they are consistent and self-confident
    d. may be persuasive if they are females

30. Survey research findings report that _____ juries ultimately reach the verdict favored by the majority on the first ballot.

    a. 9 out of 10   c. 5 out of 10
    b. 7 out of 10   d. 3 out of 10

31. In terms of the number of people who deliberate, jury research suggests that

    a. six heads are better than twelve
    b. twelve heads are better than one
    c. six males are better than nine females
    d. one head is better than twelve

32. What criticism has been made of the use of six-member juries instead of twelve-member juries?

    a. six-member juries are less likely to take their task seriously
    b. six-member juries are less likely to embody a community's diversity
    c. six-member juries are more likely to be hung juries
    d. six-member juries are more likely to become dominated by an authoritarian individual

33. Studies comparing twelve-member juries with six-member juries indicate that

    a.   twelve-member juries are likely to elicit more balanced participation per juror than are six-member juries

    b.   twelve-member juries elicit more total deliberation than six-member juries do

    c.   six-member juries tend to take their task more seriously than twelve-member juries do

    d.   twelve-member juries are significantly more likely to convict a defendant than are six-member juries

34. According to the text, simulated juries

    a.   can help us formulate theories we can use to interpret the more complex world

    b.   are almost identical to real juries so that we can readily generalize from one to the other

    c.   have been viewed by the majority of Supreme Court judges as valuable in predicting the behavior of actual juries

    d.   have mundane but not experimental realism

35. Whose eyewitness testimony is probably the most reliable?

    a.   Thressa's report immediately after a bank robbery. She was simply asked by police to tell in her own words what happened.

    b.   Sheryl's testimony about a grocery store hold-up. She has been interviewed eight times by the prosecuting attorney before appearing in court.

    c.   David's testimony about a car accident. He has been interviewed three times by the defense attorney before his court appearance.

    d.   Susan's report immediately after observing an attempted rape. She was asked very specific questions by the police, who believed they already had a suspect in custody.

36. Attorney Johnson will be defending James S., who is accused of raping a 22-year-old woman. Who of the following jurors is likely to be least sympathetic to his client's case?

    a.   John, a 40-year-old plumber who once served a sentence for burglary

    b.   Todd, a 22-year-old college student who is a political liberal

    c.   Wilma, a 42-year-old mother of two who tends to be authoritarian

    d.   Rita, a 32-year-old television executive who opposes the death penalty

37. Attorney Miller is defending Mary, a 20-year-old college student, who is being tried for failing to pay income tax. What should she do to boost Mary's chances of being acquitted?

    a.   select Bill and Philip who are also college students to serve as jurors

    b.   have Mary appear in court as attractively dressed as possible

    c.   select jurors who oppose the death penalty

    d.   she should do all of the above

38. You have just been appointed to serve as a new county judge. You are concerned about the effect inadmissible evidence may have on the jury in an upcoming trial of a case involving rape. You anticipate that the defense attorney will seek to introduce evidence regarding the victim's prior sexual history. To minimize the impact of such evidence on the jury, you should

    a.   say nothing about such inadmissible evidence to the jury
    b.   remind the jury before the trial that the victim's previous sexual history is irrelevant
    c.   only tell the jury that the evidence is inadmissible after the defense attempts to introduce it
    d.   ask the defendant to refute any damaging evidence about her previous sexual history

39. A twelve-member jury has heard all the evidence in a child abuse case and is beginning to deliberate. At the outset five favor acquittal of the defendant and seven favor conviction. Based on research in the text, the jury will probably

    a.   be unable to reach a verdict and be a hung jury
    b.   bring in a guilty verdict
    c.   vote for acquittal
    d.   vote for acquittal if the defendant is female and for conviction if the defendant is male

40. After hearing evidence in a murder trial, twelve jurors tend to believe the evidence is insufficient to convict the 25-year-old Black defendant. According to the group polarization hypothesis, after the jurors deliberate

    a.   they will be more convinced the defendant is guilty
    b.   they will be more convinced the evidence is insufficient to convict
    c.   they will be evenly split with some convinced he is guilty and others convinced he is innocent
    d.   they will be split with a minority favoring acquittal and the majority favoring conviction

SHORT ESSAY QUESTIONS

Answer the following questions in the space provided.

1. Briefly explain how error may creep into eyewitness testimony.

2. Explain how error in eyewitness testimony might be reduced.

3. Identify two defendant characteristics that may influence jurors' judgments.

4. What strategies can be used to minimize, or even eliminate, the effect of inadmissible evidence on jurors' judgments?

5. What does research indicate regarding the effects of jurors' own characteristics on their verdicts?

6. Briefly give two examples of how juries are swayed by the same influences that bear upon other types of groups.

7. Discuss the value of simulated juries as well as their possible limitations.

ANSWER KEY

Chapter Review

1. influence

2. persuasive
   inaccurate
   accuracy

3. memories
   Retelling
   please
   believe
   feedback

4. train
   false
   eyewitnesses'

5. biases
   attractive
   similar
   evidence

6. pretrial
   inadmissible
   added

7. Forewarning
   Videotaping

8. evidence
   instructions
   verdicts
   selection
   evidence

9. close
   death
   authoritarian

10. three
    95

11. two-thirds
    hung

12. consistent
    defections
    male
    high

13. stronger
    lenient
    polarization

14. more
    better
    informational

15. six-person
    consensus
    minority

Matching Terms

1. i
2. k
3. f
4. l
5. d
6. j

7. c
8. g
9. b
10. e
11. h
12. a

True-False Review

1.	F	14.	F
2.	T	15.	T
3.	T	16.	T
4.	F	17.	T
5.	T	18.	F
6.	T	19.	T
7.	T	20.	T
8.	T	21.	T
9.	F	22.	T
10.	F	23.	T
11.	T	24.	T
12.	F	25.	F
13.	T		

Multiple-Choice Practice Test

1.	b	21.	b
2.	a	22.	a
3.	b	23.	b
4.	d	24.	c
5.	d	25.	c
6.	c	26.	d
7.	b	27.	a
8.	b	28.	b
9.	a	29.	c
10.	d	30.	a
11.	b	31.	b
12.	a	32.	b
13.	d	33.	b
14.	a	34.	a
15.	b	35.	a
16.	a	36.	c
17.	a	37.	d
18.	b	38.	b
19.	c	39.	a
20.	b	40.	b

MODULE C

SOCIAL PSYCHOLOGY AND THE SUSTAINABLE FUTURE

CHAPTER OBJECTIVES

After completing your study of this chapter you should be able to:

1. Discuss the nature of the global crisis.

2. Identify two different routes to sustainable lifestyles.

3. Describe the relationship between materialism and well-being.

4. Discuss how our capacity for adaptation and tendency to make social comparisons explain the psychology of consumption.

5. Explain psychology's potential contributions to a sustainable future.

CHAPTER REVIEW

Supply the words necessary to complete each of the following statements.

THE GLOBAL CRISIS

1. As we began a new millennium we faced the _____ of times and the _____ of times. Food production had dramatically _____ and in most Western countries jobless and welfare roles had _____. At the same time, however, world _____ was projected to increase and economic growth was increasing _____.

2. One route to a sustainable future is through increasing technological _____ and agricultural _____. A second route is through reduced _____. For example, one proposal is to tax people on the basis of what they _____ rather than on the basis of what they _____.

THE SOCIAL PSYCHOLOGY OF MATERIALISM AND SIMPLICITY

3. In the 1970s and 1980s materialism _____, most clearly in the United
    States. New American collegians now rank becoming "very well-off financially" as their
    _____ objective. However, in the United States, Canada, and Europe, the
    correlation between income and personal happiness is _____. Compared to
    1957, today's Americans are twice as _____ and _____ happier.

4. The _____-level phenomenon is our tendency to adapt to a given level of
    _____ and react to changes from that level.

5. Much of life revolves around social _____. The frequent result is
    relative _____.

TOWARD SUSTAINABLE CONSUMPTION

6. More earth-friendly behavior will result from public policies that give incentive for
    _____, from persuasive appeals that elicit _____ to specific
    behaviors, and from changing "me" thinking to "_____" thinking and present
    thinking to _____ thinking.

7. Recent surveys suggest the beginnings of a decline in _____ values. From
    1994 to 1998, the percent of Americans feeling a need to "experience _____
    growth" increased dramatically.

8. Psychology's studies of the good life point to the importance of _____
    relationships, a hope-filled _____, positive traits, and engaging
    _____. .

MATCHING TERMS

Write the letter of the correct term from the right before the appropriate number on the left.

_____ 1. So absorbed in an activity we lose consciousness of self and time.

_____ 2. New collegians rank this as their most important objective.

_____ 3. The belief that there is a connection between wealth and well-being feeds this.

_____ 4. The frequent result of upward social comparison.

_____ 5. Expenditures rise to meet income.

_____ 6. Biologically productive space people in different countries require to produce what they consume and to absorb their. waste.

_____ 7. Elements of a genuinely good life.

_____ 8. Is rising among young Americans.

_____ 9. Our feelings of satisfaction and dissatisfaction are relative to our prior achievements.

a. adaptation-level phenomenon

b. "ecological footprints"

c. relative deprivation

d. flow

e. Parkinson's second law

f. "being very well off financially"

g. "cycle of work and spend"

h. volunteerism

i. close relationships, faith, engaging activity

TRUE-FALSE REVIEW

Circle T if the statement is true and F if it is false.

T F   1. Since 1960, world population has tripled while food production has only doubled.

T F   2. As we entered the new millennium, the price of cars, air travel, and hamburgers were at record inflation-adjusted lows.

T F   3. Everyone's consuming like today's Americans and Canadians would require the natural resources of three earths.

T F   4. A century ago, the leading causes of death were accidents and cancer.

T F   5. In only a few countries have fertility rates dropped to replacement levels.

T F   6. Asians now buy more cars than Western Europeans and North Americans together.

T F   7. At the present rate of destruction, according to one expert, half the earth's plant and animal species could be extinct within a century.

T F   8. The earth seems capable of permanently supporting five billion people consuming as do today's Western Europeans and North Americans.

T F   9. One route to a sustainable future is through increasing technological efficiency and agricultural productivity.

T F 10. Thanks to family planning efforts, the world's population growth rate has decelerated especially in developed nations.

T F 11. To reduce consumption, Robert Frank proposes that we tax people on what they spend rather than on what they earn.

T F 12. The text states that public consciousness is always very slow to change.

T F 13. Post-1960 American life has been marked by rising individualism and less communal engagement.

T F 14. Volunteerism among young Americans is now rising.

T F 15. In 1996 average Americans indicated that they needed an annual income of $60,000 to fulfill their dreams.

T F 16. American college students now rank "raising a family" as their number one objective.

T F 17. In the United States, Canada, and Europe, the correlation between income and personal happiness is weak.

T F 18. Very rich people are significantly happier than the average person.

T F 19. Americans reporting themselves "very happy" declined slightly between 1957 and 1998.

T F 20. Economic growth in affluent societies has provided no apparent boost to human morale.

T F 21. The adaptation-level phenomenon suggests that we can learn to adjust to a simplified way of living.

T F 22. The concept of relative deprivation refers to the perception that yesterday's luxuries are today's necessities.

T F 23. Gallup reported that from 1994 to 1998 the percentage of Americans feeling a need to "experience spiritual growth" declined significantly.

T F 24. Compared to those who never attend, those who attend church regularly are less likely to declare themselves as being very happy.

T F 25. Most people are happier gardening than power boating.

MULTIPLE-CHOICE PRACTICE TEST

Circle the correct letter.

1. Since 1960, _____ has increased and _____ have decreased.

   a. inflation-adjusted price of milk; drunken driving fatalities
   b. hard liquor consumption; inflation-adjusted prices of cars and hamburgers
   c. food production; welfare rolls
   d. the rate of inflation; stock market prices

2. Studies of world population indicate that

   a. fertility rates have dropped to replacement levels only in North America
   b. in developing countries birth rates have fallen too little to preclude rapid population growth
   c. world population is projected to reach 12 billion by 2050
   d. once replacement level birth rates are reached, world population immediately stops increasing

3. Studies of economic growth and consumption indicate that

   a. Western Europeans and North Americans together buy more cars than the rest of the world combined
   b. global warming is causing the world's forest cover to increase dramatically
   c. at the present rate of destruction all the earth's plant and animal species will be extinct within a century
   d. the earth is capable of permanently supporting only two billion people consuming as do today's Western Europeans and North Americans

4. "Ecological footprints" refers to

   a. the destruction of animal life resulting from the loss of forest cover
   b. the biologically productive space people in different nations require to produce what they consume and to absorb their wastes
   c. the impact of ecosystem destruction on the stocks of the 10 major fish species
   d. the worldwide impact of both beneficial and destructive human activity on the physical and social environment

5. The text suggests that plausible future technologies include

   a. cars that run on water
   b. washing machines that consume no water, heat, or soap
   c. edible plants that require no nutrients to grow
   d. shoes and clothes that never show wear

6. If birth rates everywhere immediately fell to replacement levels,

   a. population growth would also immediately stop
   b. total population would immediately begin a slow decline
   c. total population would immediately begin a rapid decline
   d. population growth would still continue for years to come

7. Birth rates have fallen where

   a. food security has improved and women have become educated and empowered
   b. employment has increased and inflation has decreased
   c. food prices have stabilized and hard liquor consumption has been controlled
   d. males are better educated and materialism declines

8. Economist Robert Frank proposes that we reduce consumption by taxing people on what they

   a. sell   c. spend
   b. earn   d. weigh

270

9. Between 1960 and the early 1990s, American life was marked by a decline in

   a. individualism
   b. materialism
   c. communal engagement
   d. depression

10. Between 1960 and the early 1990s, American life was marked by an increase in

    a. teen suicide
    b. carpooling
    c. volunteering
    d. charitable contributions

11. In 1996, when the Roper Organization asked Americans what annual income they needed to fulfill their dreams, the average American answered

    a. $50,000
    b. $70,000
    c. $90,000
    d. $110,000

12. At the beginning of the new millennium, surveys indicate that _____ is declining and _____ is rising.

    a. teen pregnancy; volunteerism among the young
    b. volunteerism among the young; teen violence
    c. teen employment; teen pregnancy
    d. teen violence; teen suicide

13. New American collegians rank _____ as their number one objective.

    a. becoming very well-off financially
    b. developing a meaningful philosophy of life
    c. helping others in difficulty
    d. raising a family

14. Research on national wealth and well-being indicates that

    a. the Bulgarians are happier than the Irish
    b. in poor countries, such as India, being relatively well off does not predict greater well-being
    c. the Swiss and Scandinavians are generally prosperous but unhappy
    d. in affluent societies, where most can afford life's necessities, affluence shows very little relationship to personal happiness

15. A survey of the *Forbes* 100 wealthiest Americans found that they are _____ happy than average.

    a. significantly more
    b. slightly more
    c. slightly less
    d. significantly less

16. From 1957 to 1998 Americans' inflation-adjusted income doubled. Americans reporting themselves "very happy"

    a. increased dramatically
    b. increased moderately

    c. increased slightly
    d. decreased slightly

17. Compared to their grandparents, today's young adults have grown up with

    a. greater happiness
    b. less affluence

    c. fewer social pathologies
    d. greater depression

18. College alumni who preferred a high income and occupational success and prestige to having very close friends and a close marriage were twice as like as their former classmates to describe themselves as "fairly" or "very"

    a. unhappy
    b. happy

    c. introverted
    d. extroverted

19. The two principles that help explain why people are not happier after attaining greater wealth are

    a. flow and relative deprivation
    b. Parkinson's second law and flow
    c. the adaptation-level phenomenon and relative deprivation
    d. the adaptation-level phenomenon and displacement

20. The tendency to adapt to a given level of stimulation and thus to notice and react to changes from that level is

    a. relative deprivation
    b. ecological footprints

    c. the adaptation-level phenomenon
    d. Parkinson's second law

21. Our tendency for social comparison frequently results in

    a. the adaptation-level phenomenon
    b. relative deprivation

    c. flow
    d. communal "we" thinking

22. Asked by Roper pollsters to identify what makes "the good life," 63 percent of Americans in 1996 said, "a lot of _____."

    a. friends
    b. leisure

    c. money
    d. books

23. In comparison to others, victims of paralyzing accidents

    a. typically experience a significant and lasting loss of life satisfaction
    b. eventually recover a normal or near-normal level of life satisfaction
    c. experience a highly fluctuating sense of psychological well-being throughout the rest of life.
    d. eventually experience a higher sense of self-esteem but a lower sense of relatedness to others

24. After a baseball player signs for $12 million a year, a $7 million teammate who has equal skill is most likely to experience

    a. flow
    b. relative deprivation
    c. reaction formation
    d. projection

25. Gallup reported that from 1994 to late 1998 the percent of Americans feeling a need to experience _____ rose from 58 to 82 percent.

    a. spiritual growth
    b. relatedness
    c. autonomy
    d. achievement

26. Marshall Dermer found that after women imagined and wrote about being burned and disfigured they

    a. became deeply depressed
    b. were more responsive to a request for help
    c. expressed greater satisfaction with their own lives
    d. experienced a significant loss in personal control

27. Csikszentmihalyi found that people are most likely to experience flow when

    a. unself-consciously absorbed in a mindful challenge
    b. involved in a passive leisure activity that requires little thought
    c. involved in intense interpersonal conflict with a close relative
    d. passing from the state of wakefulness to sleep

28. Most people are happier when _____ than when _____.

    a. gardening; power boating
    b. power boating; gardening
    c. watching TV; talking to friends
    d. watching TV; power boating

29. People are much likelier to declare themselves "very happy" if they

    a. are highly educated
    b. have intimate friendships
    c. are physically attractive
    d. have many children

30. In comparison to those who never attend religious services, those who attend multiple times weekly are more likely to declare themselves

    a. very happy
    b. depressed

    c. pessimistic
    d. shy

31. What personal trait has been positively related to happiness?

    a. self-esteem
    b. introversion

    c. conscientiousness
    d. passivity

32. The text suggests that more earth-friendly behavior will arise from changing _____ thinking to _____ thinking.

    a. pessimistic; optimistic
    b. future; present

    c. analytical; holistic
    d. "me"; "we"

33. Economic growth and increased consumption has been accompanied by increases in

    a. the polar ice caps
    b. droughts

    c. forest cover
    d. stocks of wild salmon and herring

34. Canadians require the equivalent of about _____ soccer fields of biologically productive space per person to produce what they consume and to absorb their waste.

    a. 2
    b. 4

    c. 8
    d. 10

35. According to the text, a blossoming turn-of-the-century social ecology movement is promoting

    a. character education in the schools
    b. "present" thinking over "future" thinking
    c. the return of mental hospital patients to community living
    d. an increase in the size of each society's "ecological footprints"

36. A 65-degree day seems warm in February but cold in July. This is best explained in terms of

    a. relative deprivation
    b. the adaptation-level phenomenon

    c. displacement
    d. Parkinson's second law

37. After Tim won one million dollars in the state lottery, he was ecstatic. After a year, however, his sense of life satisfaction returned to what it was before he won. This change in Tim's feelings can best be explained in terms of

  a. relative deprivation
  b. flow
  c. the adaptation-level phenomenon
  d. opponent-process theory

38. Maria was happy with her grade of "C" on her social psychology test until she learned that all her classmates received "A's" or "B's." The shift in Maria's feelings is best explained in terms of

  a. Parkinson's second law
  b. the adaptation-level phenomeon
  c. reaction formation
  d. relative deprivation

39. Wilbert's leisure activities include watching television, woodcarving, power boating, and sitting alone in the woods. Research suggest he is most likely to experience "flow" when

  a. daydreaming in the woods
  b. power boating
  c. woodcarving
  d. watching television

40. Michelle is a saleswoman who is depressed because recently she was denied a promotion. To increase her happiness with life, Michelle should

  a. imagine what her life would be like if she received a paralyzing physical injury
  b. compare her life with the co-worker who actually received the promotion
  c. recall moments from her early childhood when she was very happy
  d. identify the negative qualities of her supervisor who denied the promotion

SHORT ESSAY QUESTIONS

Answer the following questions in the space provided.

1. Briefly describe the causes of the present global crisis.

2. Discuss two different routes to sustainable lifestyles.

3. Cite the evidence for increased materialism and describe the relationship between wealth and well being.

4. Briefly expalin the adaptation-level phenomenon and relative deprivation.

5. Identify the factors that seem to be associated with a genuinely good life

<u>ANSWER KEY</u>

Chapter Review

1. best
   worst
   increased
   decreased
   population
   consumption

2. efficiency
   productivity
   consumption
   spend
   earn

3. increased
   first
   weak
   rich
   no

4. adaptation
   stimulation

5. comparison
   deprivation

6. conservation
   commitments
   we
   future

7. materialist
   spiritual

8. close
   faith
   activity

Matching Terms

1. d
2. f
3. g
4. c
5. e

6. b
7. i
8. h
9. a

True-False Review

1.	F	14.	T
2.	T	15.	F
3.	T	16.	F
4.	F	17.	T
5.	F	18.	F
6.	T	19.	T
7.	T	20.	T
8.	F	21.	T
9.	T	22.	F
10.	T	23.	F
11.	T	24.	F
12.	F	25.	T
13.	T		

Multiple-Choice Practice Test

1.	c	21.	b
2.	b	22.	c
3.	d	23.	b
4.	b	24.	b
5.	b	25.	a
6.	d	26.	c
7.	a	27.	a
8.	c	28.	a
9.	c	29.	b
10.	a	30.	a
11.	c	31.	a
12.	a	32.	d
13.	a	33.	b
14.	d	34.	d
15.	b	35.	a
16.	d	36.	b
17.	d	37.	c
18.	a	38.	d
19.	c	39.	c
20.	c	40.	a